Tracing Southern Storytelling
in Black and White

Tracing Southern Storytelling in Black and White

Sarah Gilbreath Ford

THE UNIVERSITY OF ALABAMA PRESS
Tuscaloosa

Copyright © 2014
The University of Alabama Press
Tuscaloosa, Alabama 35487-0380
All rights reserved
Manufactured in the United States of America

∞

Typeface: Goudy and Frutiger
Cover design: Mary Elizabeth Watson

The paper on which this book is printed meets the minimum requirements of American National Standard for Information Sciences—Permanence of Paper for Printed Library Materials, ANSI Z39.48-1984.

Library of Congress Cataloging-in-Publication Data

Ford, Sarah Gilbreath, 1968–
    Tracing southern storytelling in black and white / Sarah Gilbreath Ford.
      pages cm
    Includes bibliographical references and index.
    ISBN 978-0-8173-1823-9 (cloth : alk. paper) — ISBN 978-0-8173-8746-4 (e book)
    1. American fiction—Southern States—History and criticism. 2. American fiction—African American authors—History and criticism. 3. American fiction—White authors—History and criticism. 4. Storytelling in literature. 5. Oral tradition—Southern States. I. Title.
    PS261.F68 2014
    813.009'975–dc23
                                                                            2014000538

To Mom and Dad

Contents

Acknowledgments

The journey from idea to book was possible only because I received generous institutional and personal support. The project benefited from research sabbaticals provided by Baylor University's College of Arts and Sciences as well as encouragement from English Department chairs Maurice Hunt and Dianna Vitanza. My incredible colleagues in the English Department provided advice during every stage of the process, and I appreciate being part of such a supportive department. I am thankful to Dan Waterman at the University of Alabama Press for his guidance and direction and for the readers of the manuscript for their time and helpful suggestions.

This project has certainly been inspired and influenced by scholarship in the field of "new southern studies," and I am grateful for the larger family of scholars working in American literature and southern literature and the feedback from colleagues at American Literature Assocation and Society for the Study of Southern Literature conferences. The scholars of the Eudora Welty society have provided a kind of academic home for me; their wisdom and encouragement have been nothing less than invaluable. I would especially like to acknowledge Rebecca Mark, David McWhirter, and Harriet Pollack, who combine collegiality and "serious daring."

My friends and family have generously listened to my ideas in their various forms and have patiently encouraged me along the way, especially my sweet friends Jerrie Callan, Mona Choucair, Lisa Shaver, and Meredith Eddins, who keep me grounded and sane. My parents, E. C. and Barbara Gilbreath, model faith, hard work, and humor in equal doses and have been a true blessing in my life. And finally, I am grateful to my son, Connor, the imp, who fills my life with joy and laughter.

Introduction

Intertwining Strings

In 1943 Eudora Welty received an odd letter. She was just starting out in her career, having published several stories in magazines, a short-story collection, and a novella. Receiving fan mail from William Faulkner, who had already published fourteen books, was certainly surprising; Welty called it "strange stuff."[1] Strange indeed, as Joan St. C. Crane explains, because "[Faulkner] was not given to writing unsolicited letters to other authors, let alone to one he knew not at all" (224). The letter is even more peculiar because Faulkner confuses her work with Zora Neale Hurston's. He wrote, "You are doing fine. You are doing all right. I read THE GILDED SIX BITS, a friend loaned me THE ROBBER BRIDEGROOM, I have just bought the collection named GREEN somthing [sic], haven't read it yet, expect nothing from it because I expect from you" (Crane 223). He had admired Welty's novella *The Robber Bridegroom* and had bought the collection *A Curtain of Green*, but his attribution of "The Gilded Six Bits" to Welty is a mistake, since Welty never wrote anything with that title. Zora Neale Hurston, however, did. As Crane points out, Hurston's story by that title appeared in the August 1933 issue of *Story* alongside Faulkner's "Artist at Home." Crane suggests that Faulkner's confusion might be due in part to the "rhyming affinity of 'Zora' with 'Eudora'" (225). His letter is random enough to suggest that it is not the carefully written prose of reflection, but a note he just dashed off. In any case, the bizarre letter is a tangible bit of evidence that Faulkner read the work of his southern contemporaries Welty and Hurston and that, moreover, he liked it.

Tracing interactions between writers is not always this easy. In this study I examine how southern writers from the end of the nineteenth century through the end of the twentieth century use oral storytelling in their written texts. In each chapter I pair a white writer with an African American writer to show that the confluence of oral tradition in southern culture happens across racial lines; this is indeed one place where we can see how culture is shared. I examine Joel Chandler Harris's Uncle Remus stories with Charles Chesnutt's Uncle Julius stories, Zora Neale Hurston's *Their Eyes Were Watching God* with William Faulkner's *Absalom, Absalom!*, Ralph Ellison's *Invisible Man* with Eudora Welty's *Losing Battles*, and Ernest Gaines's *A Gathering of Old Men* with Ellen Douglas's *Can't Quit You, Baby*.

The connections between white and African American writers present a relatively new field of scholarship. Less than two decades ago Toni Morrison wrote in *Playing in the Dark: Whiteness and the Literary Imagination* that literary historians and critics were operating under the assumption that "traditional, canonical American literature is free of, uninformed, and unshaped by the four-hundred-year-old presence of, first, Africans, and then African Americans in the United States. It assumes that this presence—which shaped the body politic, the Constitution, and the entire history of the culture—has had no significant place or consequence in the origin and development of that culture's literature" (4–5). Morrison's call for scholars to see "the contemplation of this black presence [as] central to any understanding of our national literature" has certainly been influential in changing the course of literary studies, but more work should be done on examining the "interrelatedness," to borrow a term from Ralph Ellison, of white and African American culture ("Change the Joke" 55). The intersections between the literary cultures of southern white and African American writers run deeper than we have yet explored. It was on the porches, in the kitchens, and on the pages of their works that these two groups exchanged not just stories but strategies for telling stories. My project examines the conversations that their works reflect, the racial mixing of oral culture.

This examination can, however, be a bit tricky; we do not always have letters to establish affinities between writers. Examining the confluences of oral tradition is a bit like studying subatomic particles; we may not see them, but we can see their effect, the traces they leave behind. The traces are like those bouncing subatomic particles in another way as well; they do not remain static lining up in a neat form one could label "influence." Instead the traces branch out in multiple and surprising ways. As a boy Joel Chandler Harris listened to the stories of African American slaves on Turner's plantation. Harris devised a structure to turn the oral stories into written ones. His use of the frame structure gave Charles Chesnutt ideas about how to record the oral stories he heard as a child, but Harris's use of a black "uncle" to tell stories to a white boy led Alice Walker to complain that her heritage was stolen. Mark Twain picked up the use of dialect from Harris, and Twain's

work impacted how Ralph Ellison and William Faulkner used oral storytelling. Twain was also influenced by his exposure to African American culture. Shelley Fisher Fishkin argues that Twain's use of the vernacular comes
from his childhood experience listening to African American storytellers:
"The voice we have come to accept as the vernacular voice in American literature—the voice with which Twain captured our national imagination in
Huckleberry Finn, and that empowered Hemingway, Faulkner, and countless
other writers in the twentieth century—is in large measure a voice that is
'black'" (4). Twain's abilities to translate the oral culture into a written medium then influences African American writers such as Ernest Gaines, who
acknowledges that Twain in addition to Faulkner helped him learn how to
rework the storytelling of his African American culture into written prose.
As Fishkin says, "Twain helped his fellow writers learn, in very practical ways,
how to write books that 'talked'" (139). These interactions are not strictly
linear, or else we might expect Welty and Hurston to have written letters to
Faulkner; instead we have networks of interaction, borrowing, and revision,
which move forward, sideways, and occasionally backward.

In writing about southern literature as a "great dialogue," Richard Gray
uses a metaphor similar to my intertwining strings in his "web of words" to
describe the interaction between voices. He borrows this image in large part
from Judith's speech in Faulkner's *Absalom, Absalom!* about the rug: "You are
born at the same time with a lot of other people, all mixed up with them,
like trying to, having to, move your arms and legs with strings only the same
strings are hitched to all the other arms and legs and the others all trying and
they dont know why either except that the strings are all in one another's way
like five or six people all trying to make a rug on the same loom only each
one wants to weave his own pattern into the rug" (100–101). This powerful
image conveys the multiplicity of voices contributing to a narrative. The particular narrative Gray targets is that of southern literature, explaining that
there is the "talk *in* southern literature, and there is the talk *of* southern literature" (*Web* 9). The talk *in* southern literature is the use of oral storytelling:
"At the heart of many works like these are speech and storytelling—the ability
to construct a very particular world out of words and to make *a* South" (10).
The talk *of* southern literature is the conversation between writers: "Along
with conversations *in* southern texts, there are also the conversations *of* and
between southern texts: as each writer struggles with the 'ugly fact' that books
come from and talk to other books." He imagines such conversations as "Arguments with the Agrarians" or "Arguments with Faulkner." I share Gray's
interest in the idea of conversations between texts; the conversation I will
examine could be entitled, echoing Fishkin's words, "How to Make Books

that Talk." For Gray these conversations tend to be arguments, just as for Judith weaving the rug is a struggle against other people. While certain issues about making books talk, such as using dialect, are potentially contentious and even explosive, my examination will also include positive connections, such as the possibility of confluence, so that we can see the full interaction of those intertwining strings; we can see, for example, not just what strategies Chesnutt borrows from Harris but what strategies Faulkner shares in common with Hurston.

Examining the talk in southern literature raises the thorny question of that adjective "southern" and the usefulness of the regional description as a container for these works. Do these writers include storytelling in their works naturally because it is part of their "southern" DNA, or are the works constructed as "southern" when readers and critics decide that the stories have a southern accent? In claiming that the "South" and "southern literature" are simply constructions, contemporary literary critics have followed the path forged by postcolonial theorists. If the nation is, as Benedict Anderson argues, an "imagined community," then the South as a region within that nation is likewise imagined. Michael Kreyling's 1998 metanarrative, *Inventing Southern Literature*, details how the field of southern literature, beginning with the Fugitive Agrarians, was constructed in the first place, thereby exposing the invention of the monolithic ideal of "southern literature." Kreyling argues that "understanding the South without attempting to understand the projects that have created, indicted, refurbished, or rebirthed it is impossible. The history of southern literature is not the history of an 'entity,' of 'fact' understood to be within time but not of time" (xviii). Patricia Yaeger's 2000 study, *Dirt and Desire: Reconstructing Southern Women's Writing*, picks up where Kreyling leaves off by offering a "counternarrative." Kreyling claims that he does not want to "dynamite the rails on which the official narrative runs" (ix), but Yaeger asks, "What can I use for nitroglycerin?" (34). The deconstruction performed by critics such as Kreyling and Yaeger has been powerful in clearing the field, and many recent critics have offered more counternarratives. Southern literature can now be any number of things, from an examination of the function of violence to a study of the "South" that includes the Caribbean. The "southern" I see in the "southern" oral storytelling I examine is not one strictly of geographical place (after all, I want to include Ralph Ellison in my study) although certainly even in imagined communities, the concept of place retains power. The construction I am offering here is one of a shared interest in both the oral storytelling present in southern white and African American cultures and in the process of translating the powerful dynamics of oral storytelling into written prose. I want to use the space provided by the deconstruction of rigid categories and suggest that we can see the light not just as particle but also as wave, that is, the confluence can show us another potential construction of what "South" can mean. Defining a study as a construction does not mean, however, that the connections are invented or wholly fictional. We can see the confluence in these works because the writers themselves have so much in common. In choosing to draw from folk tradition and use oral storytelling, all of these writers are speaking back to and thus rewriting the construction of their literature as "southern."[2]

The writers have their work cut out for them, however, as the construction they are speaking back to is very powerful. The particular identity of the "South" as connected to slavery and the Civil War and as shaped by violence and racism is one of those grand metanarratives that, although constructed, remains attractive. Its force comes from the role that the metanarrative of the South plays in the larger construction of American national identity. Jennifer Greeson, in studying the early conception of the South, finds that "what remains constant across U.S. history is the conceptual structure provided to us by our South: it is an *internal other* for the nation, an intrinsic part of the national body that nonetheless is differentiated and held apart from the whole" (1). It can therefore play the part of "a backward glance, a conduit to the American colonial past against which [writers] may gauge the rise of the independent, developing republic" (4). Leigh Anne Duck locates a similar construction in the modern time period: "The representation of African American oppression as a specifically southern problem cast[s] the conflict between egalitarian democracy and white supremacy as a dichotomy between national and regional practice" (23). And Teresa Goddu, in explaining how the gothic form "like race, seems to become most visible in a Southern locale," finds again that it is the South's role in its relationship to American identity that is crucial: "The South's oppositional image—its gothic excesses and social transgressions—has served as the nation's safety valve. As the repository for everything the nation is *not*, the South purges the nation of its contrary impulses. More perceived idea than social reality, the imaginary South functions as the nation's 'dark' other" ("Ghost" 232).

Although affixing the regional adjective "southern" to any of the works I examine could constrict their potential meanings, each of these works seems to play right into the construction of "southern" that Greeson, Duck, and Goddu detail, as each depicts characters who are only a step or two away from the slavery/Civil War nexus that defines that backward and deviant South. Harris's and Chesnutt's narrators tell stories from their experiences in slavery. Faulkner's Quentin complains about the ghosts of the Civil War haunting him. Hurston's Janie hears stories about the position of black women in slavery from her grandmother. Ellison's narrator has a panic attack when he sees free papers among an elderly couple's belongings because he thinks it has surely been longer ago than that. Welty's family tells the story of their beloved Granny Vaughn witnessing Grant firing a cannonball at the family home. Gaines's old men not only still live on the same plantations that their forefathers and foremothers worked, they meet at a cemetery, highlighting their close connection to the previous enslaved generation. Douglas's Tweet tells the story of her grandfather receiving a pension from fighting in the Civil War while Cornelia's reaction, that he surely could not be that old, echoes the narrator's in *Invisible Man*. In each work the Civil War and/or the experience of slavery looms in the background, rendering the texts clearly within that construction of southern literature as backward, or at least backward looking.

The decision by these writers to dip into the pot of folk culture and use oral storytelling in their works could also further mark the texts as backward looking, but only if we do not recognize the use of oral storytelling as a strategy, as a way of performing regional identity, that changes it in the process and allows the writers to speak back to that rigid and narrow construction of what southern means. When Merrill Maguire Skaggs asks why southern literature is connected to oral tradition more than midwestern or rural New England literature, her answer is that "this semblance of oral storytelling was a carefully cultivated (and artificially contrived) literary technique. . . . But however that might be, southern writers developed this narrative technique, using double narrators and the 'frame' device, which *seems* simply the record of a conversation. The conversational tone, the oral tradition apparently behind the story, is the development of a literary tradition" (195). The writers choose to use oral storytelling and use it, as Skaggs points out, as a cultivated literary device despite the possibility of negative associations. I must, however, include a caveat about that level of choice. Writers (unfortunately) do not write in an artistic vacuum where every choice is decided by aesthetic principles. They need readers to buy books. Charles Chesnutt, for example, found success writing local color stories, which played off of oral storytelling and relied heavily on dialect. Richard Brodhead argues that with the exceptions of Henry James and William Dean Howells, "every other writer of [the post–Civil War time period] who succeeded in establishing himself as a writer did so through the regional form" (*Cultures* 116). Although the public's appetite allowed Chesnutt to publish his work, Brodhead explains the dark side of this interest: "[Regionalism's] place of cultural production would clearly seem to link regionalism with an elite need for the primitive made available as a leisure outlet" (132). When Chesnutt tried to publish his writings about the situation of mixed-race people in American society sans storytelling and dialect, he was not successful. Choice takes place within social and financial constraints, although most critics agree that Chesnutt was able to write radically subversive texts while appeasing his white audience.

While choice is certainly shaped by historical context, when these writers chose to use oral storytelling, they injected a different dynamic into their work. When Jennifer Greeson examines the prevalence of the concept of the South in American literary history, she asks, "What is our South good for?" (2). The concept's sheer endurance begs the question of its attractiveness and utility. I explore a similar question here about these writers' use of oral storytelling. My study includes white and African American writers, men and women, writing from 1881 to 1989, who all employ oral storytelling. Not only must it be good for something, it must also be quite different from its typical construction as nostalgic, conservative, and backward looking. In Patricia Yaeger's desire to explode the traditional tracks of southern literature, she includes storytelling on the list of the "truisms" she finds uninteresting (11). I would argue that the prevalence of oral storytelling in southern fiction suggests that the writers themselves find something quite interesting. In examining "why has storytelling—particularly oral, folk, or traditional storytelling—become so prominent a topic in current fiction?" Jay Clayton finds that storytelling can be empowering and experimental (376). This seems to be something southern writers, coming from cultures rich with oral traditions, already know.

Oral storytelling proves to be an empowering and useful tool for all of the writers I examine because its dynamics differ from those of written prose. Walter Ong's influential studies, the 1977 *Interfaces of the Word: Studies in the Evolution of Consciousness and Culture* and the 1982 *Orality and Literacy: The Technologizing of the Word*, paved the way for scholars to understand the dramatic differences between oral and written cultures. The key difference is the presence of a live audience for an oral story. Whereas the "writer's audience is always a fiction," Ong explains that an oral storytelling performance "is always a live interaction between a speaker and his audience. It is necessarily participatory at least to the extent that the way the audience reacts determines to a degree the way the speaker performs, and vice versa" (*Interfaces* 53, 277). This interaction completely changes the dynamics of a narrative because the listener can shape, interrupt, or even at times take over the storytelling. Unlike a written text where the author has the sole authority (or at least the semblance of it, to give credit to reader response theory), oral storytelling is a joint venture.[3] This participatory quality is a key ingredient scholars have identified in southern white and African American narratives. In an examination of twentieth-century black fiction, John Callahan identifies this interaction as "call-and-response": "In the African-American grain, stories were told in unceasing collaboration between the storyteller and his audience, the black community. Call-and-response was so fundamental to the form and meaning of the tale that anyone, black or white, allowed into the circle was bound to become a participant as well as a witness" (27). Trudier Harris places the emphasis on audience squarely on southern ground: "Whatever else cultural analysts may conclude about the South, they generally agree on one thing: southerners like to talk. Talking presupposes givers and takers, speakers and audiences, tellers and listeners" (56).

The interaction these critics see as key to oral storytelling may be more lacking in the novel than in other prose forms. Walter Benjamin's theories about the differences between storytelling and the novel seem to parallel Ong's distinctions between oral and written texts, although Benjamin comes to the issue from a different angle and restricts his ideas to literature. Benjamin finds that "the earliest indication of a process whose end is the decline of storytelling is the rise of the novel at the beginning of modern times" (146). He singles out the novel from other prose forms such as the "fairy tale, the legend, even the novella" because the novel "neither comes from oral tradition nor enters into it" (146). The key difference is interaction versus isolation: "The storyteller takes what he tells from experience—his own or that reported by others. And he in turn makes it the experience of those who are listening to his tale. The novelist has secluded himself. The birthplace of the novel is the individual in his isolation, the individual who can no longer speak of his concerns in exemplary fashion, who himself lacks counsel and can give none" (146). Oral storytelling, with listeners in attendance, allows the interaction that written texts, and perhaps as Benjamin argues the modern novel most of all, do not.

This interaction causes oral narratives to be spontaneous, unlike written narratives where the words are fixed on a page. Ong writes, "Print encourages a sense of closure, a sense that what is found in a text has been finalized, has reached a state of completion" (*Orality* 132). Julius Lester, in discussing his modern rewriting of the Uncle Remus tales, explains the difference: "Literature exists on the page. Once it takes that form, it cannot be changed. A story is elastic; it is recreated by the tongue of each teller and with each telling" ("Storyteller's" 69). The effect of print's sense of closure is, according to Ong, a kind of distancing from the reader as the "verbal creation comes more and more to be regarded as an object" (*Interfaces* 280). The focus of the reader's attention becomes the object itself whereas the focus in oral narrative shifts to the construction of the narrative and the person doing the constructing. Allen Tate noted in 1959 this particular trait of southern discourse: "The Southerner always talks to somebody else, and this somebody else, after varying intervals, is given his turn; but the conversation is always among rhetoricians; that is to say, the typical Southern conversation is not going anywhere; it is not about anything. *It is about the people who are talking*" (584). Audiences for oral storytelling may already know the story being told, so they focus on the performance.

This performance may, however, be followed by others, another implication of lack of closure inherent in oral narratives. Ong explains that sound is fundamentally an "on-going event"; you cannot pause on a sound or fix it in space (*Orality* 161). Oral storytelling is likewise potentially an ongoing event because that participatory listener might decide to become a teller. Theresa Melendez explains that "only in oral literature is the perceiver of a work a potential author of that work. . . . Thus the communication of oral literature is an open system at the level not only of interpretation (which may be true for written texts) but also of generation within the social group in which it is reproduced" (81). This live audience together with the open quality of the narrative and the focus on performance give oral storytelling quite different dynamics from those of written narratives. Although not all of these dynamics are present in every text I will examine, they provide possibilities for writers to inject more fluid dynamics into written prose.

The key is getting these dynamics into writing. The writers are not engaged in live storytelling performances with flesh-and-blood audiences, and Ong's saying that "the writer's audience is always a fiction" is certainly even true here, as much as the writers pull from their oral culture roots. But even Ong at times in his studies talks about the "residual" orality in the written works of cultures with thriving oral traditions and offers one way in which the divide can be crossed: "Nor is orality ever completely eradicable: reading a text oralizes it" (*Orality* 175). What these writers attempt to do is lead their readers to oralize the texts. They have to come up with strategies to mimic oral performances through the static written words on the page. The most prevalent strategy is the use of a character's voice written in dialect so that the narrator appears to be "talking" instead of writing. The Russian Formalists labeled this technique *skaz*,[4] and Mikhail Bakhtin explains that "in the majority of cases *skaz* is above all an orientation toward *someone else's speech*, and only then, as a consequence, toward oral speech" (*Problems* 191). The use of *skaz* allows the author to insert a storyteller, who is, as Bakhtin notes, "after all, not a literary person," and to provide the illusion of that spontaneous oral performance. Writers then add to this illusion by using other strategies, such as addressing the reader in second person, positioning characters as listeners, or using postmodern metanarrative. Their texts then have the semblance of orality.

Perhaps the best way to describe books that talk is "speakerly," a term coined by Henry Louis Gates Jr. in his examination of Hurston's work.[5] For Gates, a "speakerly" text is "a profoundly lyrical, densely metaphorical, quasi-musical, privileged black oral tradition on the one hand, and a received but not yet fully appropriated standard English literary tradition on the other hand" (174). Gates identifies the combination and tension between the spoken and written words but sees it refracted also by race, the tension between the "black vernacular and the literate white text" (131). This separation works to unpack the complexities of Hurston's writing. John Callahan poses a similar argument for the African American writers he examines, showing their attempt to "conjure the spoken word into symbolic existence on the page" (14). What Gates and Callahan claim for these texts, however, I would like to extend to all of the narratives I examine, which either derive from the African American oral culture Gates and Callahan explore or from the southern white oral culture with which I will argue it shares some cultural DNA. We can best think about these talking books as hybrids; they play in a middle ground between the oral and written.

Of course the southern writers did not invent this middle ground; it is indeed that Russian word *skaz* that first describes the technique. Moreover, the technique of the frame tale that some of these writers use to pose characters as listeners goes all the way back to the Middle Ages and Chaucer's pilgrims.[6] These eight writers, though, perhaps because of that residual but thriving southern oral culture, are particularly invested in oral storytelling and use it to change the narrative dynamics of their fiction. Their experiments in trying to occupy this middle ground are radical, suggesting that oral storytelling is not (just) an old weapon to conserve the status quo and bask in nostalgia. The juncture of oral storytelling and written word is the place where these narratives become fluid, communal, and dynamic.

This juncture also leads to the confluences I will examine in the work of these eight writers. The confluences occur not just due to the borrowing back and forth that happens in that constructed space of the South but also because of shared historical contexts. Just as literary critics have been busy deconstructing the "southern" in southern literature, historians have been studying how regionalism is constructed and reconstructed in American culture. Although the concept of regions, including the South, seems to persist through time, in certain decades the concept carries more weight. Historians Michael Steiner and David Wrobel describe regionalism as having an "episodic history": "As a largely unconscious source of identity, region-alism has been a compelling force throughout American history, but at cer-tain points it becomes a *self-conscious* concern—a cause and a rallying cry" (6). The particular time periods historians find regionalism most prevalent are the 1880s–90s, the 1930s, and the 1970s–80s.[7] Interestingly, these three pe-riods line up roughly with the texts in this study. Joel Chandler Harris and Charles Chesnutt wrote at the turn of the century. William Faulkner's and Zora Neale Hurston's texts are from the 1930s. Although Ralph Ellison and Eudora Welty wrote later, they both set their works in the 1930s. Ernest Gaines and Ellen Douglas set their novels in the 1960s and 1970s. In the individual chapters I will trace the impact of regionalist ideas in these time periods, specifically local color at the turn of the century, the Works Prog-ress Administration (WPA) in the 1930s, and postmodernism in the 1970s.

The shared historical contexts lead to confluences between writers in the ways they use oral storytelling. Joel Chandler Harris and Charles Chesnutt, writing in a post–Civil War America, use oral storytelling as a way of form-ing communities. The humor in their stories bonds the insiders who get the jokes and then laugh together at the cruel ironies of the slave system. Zora Neale Hurston and William Faulkner, writing at the height of modernism, depict characters striving to establish carefully ordered paradises based on ra-cial exclusion. The oral storytelling in their works questions the master narra-tives needed to keep the boundaries firm. Ralph Ellison and Eudora Welty, looking back on the 1930s, both depict the plight of rural folk culture bat-tling for survival against the forces of modernism. Oral storytelling becomes a useful tool of subversion as the folk use their humor to undermine the se-rious business of progress. Ellen Douglas and Ernest Gaines set their novels in post–civil rights America. The problems of segregation are, however, still pressing, and oral storytelling becomes a bridge for crossing racial lines.

What if Welty had written back to Faulkner? What would she have said? What if Hurston had written to them both? Unfortunately these answers must remain in the realm of imagination. What we can do is follow the traces of the confluence and construct conversations. Salman Rushdie, speaking about the difficulty of "reconciling old and new," says that "*Melange*, hotch-potch, a bit of this and a bit of that is *how newness enters the world*" (394). The "hotchpotch" in these texts is a bit oral and a bit written, and the oral story-telling itself also contains a mélange of cultural traditions. Oral storytelling as an everyday, ordinary, low form of culture can be especially sly about the mixing of its cultural parentage. Stories are told in beauty parlors, at kitchen tables, and on the street in words that exist momentarily and are not sub-ject to the scrutiny of official written texts. The stories are passed down and around and through individuals, communities, and occasionally over race lines. When the story is retold by a different person in a different context, it becomes part of the cultural atmosphere that these writers then draw from to create a middle ground between the oral and the written. Newness enters the world. As scientists open up new realms of the universe, on both the quantum and nuclear scales, they have not discovered static, sturdy building blocks but an expanding universe with whirling particles, all connected by dancing, vibrating strings of energy. The paths of oral storytelling resemble a web of dancing strings. This study will trace the story of how some of these strings intertwine.

1
Getting the Joke

Joel Chandler Harrris's *Uncle Remus: His Songs and Sayings* and Charles Chesnutt's *The Conjure Woman*

In an 1895 essay, "How to Tell a Story," Mark Twain explains how a story "ought to be told" by focusing on the genre of the humorous story (3). To Twain, the humorous story is "art" and distinctly American; he then assigns the comic story to England and the witty story to France. It is certainly no secret which of the three he sees as superior as he discusses the difficulty of telling a humorous story well but claims that even a machine could tell a comic story. The underlying difference between the humorous story and its European rivals is that it is oral, whereas the other two are primarily written. The humorous story depends on the "*manner* of the telling; the comic story and the witty story upon the *matter*" (3). Twain emphasizes this oral foundation when he says, "The art of telling a humorous story—understand I mean by word of mouth, not print—was created in America, and has remained at home" (4). Twain's guidelines for a good story certainly describe the stories of Joel Chandler Harris and Charles Chesnutt, contemporaries of Twain. Both Harris's character Uncle Remus and Chesnutt's character Uncle Julius fit the role of the artist that Twain outlines, as they are masters of the manner of the story and the dynamics of the storytelling performance. That the masters of this distinctly American form are African American is indicative of the cultural exchange embedded in the history of oral storytelling. Through the Uncle Remus stories, Harris, a white writer, employs a black narrator to tell African American folktales, thus influencing Chesnutt, an African American writer, to create his own version of a black "uncle," Julius, telling African American folktales to a fictional white audience.

In telling stories based on African American folklore to white audiences, Uncle Remus and Uncle Julius introduce in print the collision between white and black storytelling traditions, although both traditions predate these written records. The black oral tradition that provides the foundation for both Harris's and Chesnutt's stories has a distant past. The antebellum oral story-telling tradition among African Americans is alluded to in numerous works, even those of apologists for slavery such as John Pendleton Kennedy in his 1853 work, *Swallow Barn*. Folklorists, however, have traced the Brer Rabbit stories Harris tells to even older traditions in Africa, evidence that slaves brought the stories to America with them. This older oral tradition was still alive and thriving when Harris decided to record some of the tales he had heard in his 1881 book.[1] White writers were experimenting with oral storytelling in the years before the Civil War in the humorous stories and sketches published in newspapers and magazines in the movement known as "southwestern humor." The writers' use of the frame tale as a method of bracketing an oral tale and their use of dialect find their way into Harris's and Chesnutt's stories, although with much different functions. The south-western humorists used the frame tale, as Hennig Cohen and William Dillingham explain, to create an "aesthetic distance" between the authors and the lower-class backwoods characters of their stories: "The Southwest humorist wanted to laugh at the earthy life around him and to enjoy it, but he did not want to be identified with it" (xxx). Using the frame structure also highlighted the difference between the narrative of the gentleman-narrator's comments written in grammatically correct prose and the embedded oral narratives told in colorful and humorous dialect.

The popularity of dialect carried over into the post–Civil War literary movement that was known as "local color." The use of dialect in local color fiction, however, was less about the bawdy humor of the lower class and more about capturing the linguistic particularities of people in a particular region. The appeal of regionalism for readers of this time period was, as Lucinda MacKethan explains, "diverse and complex," but local color fiction mainly "seemed to feed the burgeoning awareness of a reconciled nation concerning sectional differences that needed new study and reinforced tolerance" (36–37). America seemed more conscious of differences stemming from regional boundaries, and Robert Bone notes the paradox that "a stronger sense of nationhood could only be attained through a greater tolerance of sectional differences" (9). Richard Brodhead's reading of the rise of regionalism, however, is much darker. Although interest in folk culture allowed writers who knew about these cultures, such as Charles Chesnutt, to be published, the public interest was not in preservation or celebration. Brodhead argues, "For the United States, regionalism's representation of vernacular cultures as enclaves of tradition insulated from larger cultural contact is palpably a fiction. This would suggest that its public function was not just to mourn lost cultures but to purvey a certain story of contemporary cultures and of the relations among them: to tell local cultures into a history of their supersession by a modern order now risen to national dominance" (*Cultures* 121). Brodhead finds that this fiction allows a kind of distancing between the superior audience and inferior storytellers (similar to the dynamics of the frame tale for the southwestern humorists) and argues that regionalism filled "an elite need for the primitive made available as leisure outlet" (132).

Although Brodhead's analysis of this power structure is persuasive, Gavin Jones argues that these were not the only dynamics at play; his work attempts to "overturn the belief that dialect functioned chiefly to uphold the dominance of an elitest ideology, that it acted solely as a reassuring means of regional nostalgia" (8). Interpreting the significance of dialect is certainly tricky; Eric Sundquist finds today's critics and readers may have a difficult time: "Modern distaste for dialect writing—in particular the justified contempt for the use of racially stereotyped dialect as a means of denigration in stories, cartoons, advertisements, and the like—has made both critics and readers reluctant to look closely at its cultural significance" (*To Wake* 303). In Harris's and Chesnutt's time dialect was not just a means for showing the inferiority of the African American culture; Jones argues its specific significance for African Americans: "Black language also encompassed the power of cultural contamination. African-American dialect was a sign of black-white intermixture; it was a hybrid form with the force to infiltrate and adulterate the dominant language" (8).

It is indeed this mixture of language through the use of oral storytelling that I find in Harris's and Chesnutt's stories. Although their works were fueled by the attention to regionalism, I will show how both authors wrote back to the historical context. The particular southern version of the local color movement was the plantation school, in which authors such as Thomas Nelson Page waxed nostalgic about the supposedly genteel life in the South before the Civil War, resulting in the "moonlight and magnolias" image of the antebellum South. Joel Chandler Harris's depiction of Uncle Remus, a contented ex-slave who still lives on the old plantation, seems to fit this pastoral vision nicely, and even Uncle Julius's characterization echoes these local color stories. Harris and Chesnutt, however, go beyond the function of recording and containing a specific slice of southern culture. Their stories are not museum pieces frozen in time to preserve a particularly saccharine depiction of southern life and race relations; they instead question, revise, and play with that image. While Harris and Chesnutt do use dialect, instead of distancing the audience from the storytelling, the orality of the language connects the reader to the story, mimicking how listeners are involved in oral storytelling performances. Harris borrows the frame tale from the southwestern humorists but moves beyond the cultural distancing the form offered to earlier writers to provide a sense of vital interaction. Chesnutt takes Harris's basic form and pushes it even further to show that the dynamic exchange of oral storytelling can form communities. The white members of the audience hearing the storytelling performance are at the beginning outsiders to its form and meaning, but as they start to understand the humor, they become insiders who get the jokes and therefore the radical critique of slavery in Uncle Julius's tales.

The potential mixed community for storytelling is even a part of Twain's analysis, although he does not acknowledge it. In "How to Tell a Story," Twain actually shows as much as he tells about the art of telling a story. He explains that the American tale is humorous and specifically oral, "word of mouth," but he shows that its origin is not so much American as African American (4). In giving an example of a humorous story, Twain tells a "negro ghost story," entitled "The Golden Arm." When he earlier tries to appear humble in claiming that he perhaps could not tell a story but he knew how a story ought to be told, he banks his expertise on having been "almost daily in the company of the most expert story-tellers for many years" (3). Shelley Fisher Fishkin has detailed how much of Twain's storytelling background came from the African Americans he knew growing up. The influence is certainly evident in this essay, as he even tells the story in dialect: "Once 'pon a time dey wuz a monsus mean man, en he live 'way out in de praire all 'lone by hisself, 'cep'n he had a wife" (10). The story includes a pause before what Twain calls the "snapper" at the end, when Twain then instructs the reader to pick a girl from the audience to frighten with the last line. The story is a performance requiring an audience to complete the joke, supporting Twain's assertion that the humorous story is at its root oral. With the reach to the audience at the end, Twain gives a lesson in how stories can walk off the page and into the audience. The snapper of Twain's essay, however, is the voice telling the story; Twain reveals that the American story speaks to its audience in "Negro" dialect. Chesnutt and Harris speak the same language and rely on their audiences to listen and to get the joke.

***

To understand how Chesnutt and Harris tell jokes to reach out and grab their audiences, we must first see their stories as written texts playing with oral storytelling. In employing frames to introduce stories, both writers highlight the orality of the stories, and, by positioning the reader as part of the audience listening to a tale "told" in dialect, the texts play with the line between the spoken and written word. They mimic active storytelling in an attempt to replicate a dynamic live performance, even though they, paradoxically, do this through written words on a page. Julius Lester, in discussing his modern version of the Uncle Remus tales, describes this paradox: "Stories from the oral tradition are not meant for the page. . . . Literature exists on the page. Once it takes that form, it cannot be changed. A story is elastic; it is recreated by the tongue of each teller and with each telling" ("Storyteller's" 69). Joel Chandler Harris and Charles Chesnutt employ the frame tale to play with this paradox, to write prose that feels more like the oral stories Lester describes as elastic and communal.[2]

Many critics and readers, however, miss one part of the equation and, especially in the case of Harris, see the texts as either purely oral or purely written. Critics who read the Uncle Remus tales as "folklore" speak of Harris as a kind of ethnographer who recorded the tales. Harris, of course, contributes to this view by using the term "folklore" and by claiming he simply wrote the tales as he heard them and that none of them were "cooked."[3] But reading the stories this way requires dismissing the frame, which provides not only unity but also context. Critics such as Robert Bone suggest that when the tale is split from the frame, the value should only be the tale: "A crucial distinction must be drawn between the kernel and the husk. It is undeniable that the external wrappings of the Brer Rabbit tales function to perpetuate the plantation myth. But the tales themselves were never tampered with. As a conscientious if amateur ethnologist, Harris respected their integrity" (23). Bone's insistence on the integrity of the tales points to the second weakness of this approach: one must rely on Harris's ability as a reporter, as Lyle Glazier does when he claims, "Harris recorded with infinite care, listening to his Negro original and recording as accurately as if he had a tape recorder, then translating the spoken into a written dialect that seems literal without appearing ridiculous" (71). Of course, we do not know how faithful Harris was to the particular African American storytellers he heard; we could only know how accurate he was if we ourselves held the tape recorder next to Harris. The use of written dialect alone suggests at least some amount of shaping of the material by Harris even if we choose to ignore the frame.

Other critics choose to ignore the oral tradition behind the stories and thus examine the written document to see what Joel Chandler Harris intended in his particular writing of the tales. Lucinda Hardwick MacKethan suggests a positive view of Harris when she argues the tales are "a black slave's dream of Arcady," which undercuts white society (70).[4] Bernard Wolfe goes to the extreme of psychoanalyzing Harris and decides he has a love/hate relationship with blacks. By looking at Joel Chandler Harris, the person, and trying to assess his biases in order to read the stories, critics are looking for authority where it does not exist. We typically consider the author to have authority over the meaning of a written text, but this construction of power does not work well for oral storytelling, where the content of the story is passed down and the role of the speaker is to determine how best to tell the story.

That the tension between oral and written is not as marked in the Chesnutt criticism is in part because the critics all seem to agree that both the frames and the stories in *The Conjure Woman*[5] provide a critique of slavery and because Chesnutt distances himself from folklore when he claims that his tales are different from Harris's because his are the "fruit of my own imagination" ("Post-Bellum" 193). He later undercuts his assertion in his essay "Superstitions and Folk-lore of the South," when he admits that a few elements of the stories he thought he had made up were actually stories he had heard as a child and were in his latent mind. How close the stories are to an actual oral tradition is then in question. Even so, Elon Kulh complains about Chesnutt's use of folklore because, he claims, Chesnutt misrepresents hoodoo, so the stories are not a true "product of oral tradition" (247). Separating what is true oral tradition and what is traditional writing is tricky business, particularly because Chesnutt blurs the line. By paying attention to the middle ground between oral storytelling and writing that the stories of both Chesnutt and Harris inhabit, I will show how they use the form of the frame tale, not to preserve oral storytelling in a static form but to mimic its active, elastic, and communal nature.

***

The obvious marker that demonstrates the writers playing with orality is their use of dialect. The framing of the stories highlights this choice by offering a contrast between the standard diction of the narrators in the frames and the creative spelling used to convey the dialect of the storytellers in the interior stories. In using dialect Harris and Chesnutt are firmly in vogue with the local colorists, who found dialect a convenient way to capture the particularities of place as well as to claim realism because that dialect more closely portrays the language people actually speak. Writers from Thomas Nelson Page to Mark Twain had to experiment with how to make the writing on the page look like the language spoken by characters. The problem, however, with the use of dialect is that the intention to show the reality of difference in language use could result in that difference marking not realism but racial disparity. Some characters' dialect matters while others' does not. While Mark Twain might inflect Huck's speech as well as Jim's (although certainly to a lesser degree), in Thomas Nelson Page's stories, the white narrator "speaks" in formal standard written English. Added to this racial distinction in dialect is the frame form Harris and Chesnutt use, which strictly separates the narrative spoken in dialect from the frame, which is not in dialect, thus separating white from black.[6] John Callahan argues that this is indeed what happens in Harris's stories: "At no point does [the narrator] turn the narrative over to Remus for longer than it takes the old man to tell and embellish a tale or two, and his third-person, standard English voice encircles both Remus's dialect and the little boy's vernacular" (34). If the dialect is preserving a local culture, the problem is that what it is preserving is difference; racism is presented as a picture postcard from the South.

But there is certainly another way to see the use of dialect: as an attempt to introduce orality to the written text, an orality necessarily inscribed in black dialect because the oral tradition Harris plays with is black. Harris's careful rendering of language points less to the inferior racial status attached to the dialect than to the marvelous sound of the language itself. That the reader is supposed to hear and enjoy the master storyteller Uncle Remus tell the stories is emphasized by the transcription of his sounds in various tales. In "The Wonderful Tar Baby Story" when Brer Rabbit comes down the road, Uncle Remus says he is "pacin'" "lippity-clippity, clippity-lippity—dez ez sassy ez a jaybird" (58). The sound of the language gives the picture of the speedy and "sassy" rabbit. When Brer Fox comes to Brer Rabbit's house to confront him about telling the neighbors that Brer Fox was "my daddy's ridin'-hoss fer thirty year," the reader hears the knock on the door: "Brer Fox knock. Nobody ans'er. Den he knock agin—blam! blam!" (68). The dialect and the inclusion of sounds heighten the illusion of orality.

The narrator even explains that Uncle Remus's language is not fully captured in print. When Brer Tarrypin convinces Brer Fox to let go of his tail, he goes to the bottom with the sound, "kerblunkity-blink!"(88). The narrator then says, "No typographical combination or description could do justice to the guttural sonorousness—the peculiar intonation—which Uncle Remus imparted to this combination" (88). The narrator again claims the inadequacy of writing when trying to express Remus's version of Tarrypin talk: "I-doom-er-ker-kum-mer-ker!" (92). At one point the little boy comes upon Remus singing a "senseless" song, which Remus then changes into "nonsense" when he hears the boy coming (133). Craig Werner writes of this passage: "Trapped within the hierarchical system which denies transcendence to the Afro-American subject, Harris can only dismiss Uncle Remus's words, albeit with a great uneasiness on his sense that the black voice signifies something unavailable to any white 'presence' in the text" (348). That unavailability might be hiding uneasiness, but if Uncle Remus's voice and dialect are signaling orality, the text seems not to dismiss but to highlight the ways the written language cannot capture Remus's voice. Like Twain's grab at the audience in his essay, the full art of the performance is more than the printed page. Dialect allows the reader to hear hints of that performance and to enjoy the sound.

In Chesnutt's stories the difference between the language of the frame and the dialect of Uncle Julius is even greater. With the ever-rational northern farmer John as the voice of the frame, the diction and sentence structure is more complex than the unnamed narrator in Harris's tales. In the first story, for example, when John explains why Annie's doctor suggests they move south, he says, "I shared, from an unprofessional standpoint, his opinion that the raw winds, and the violent changes of temperature that characterized the winters in the region of the Great Lakes tended to aggravate my wife's difficulty, and would undoubtedly shorten her life if she remained exposed to them" (*Conjure Tales* 1). His elevated language makes, then, a striking contrast to Uncle Julius when John meets him: "Well, suh, you is a stranger ter me, en I is a stranger ter you, en we is bofe strangers ter one anudder, but 'f I 'uz in yo' place, I wouldn' buy dis vimya'd" (11). John even has a hard time understanding Julius and asks for clarification when Julius says the "ole vimya'd is goophered" (11). Charles Chesnutt himself comments on the distinction between the "naive and simple" stories told in "Negro dialect, put in the mouth of an old Negro gardener," and "the introductions to the stories, which were written in the best English I could command" ("Post-Bellum" 193). Because Chesnutt works in the plantation tale genre, he runs the same risk that Harris does that his use of dialect will be read as inflecting the racial inferiority of his black characters. Chesnutt certainly wanted to distance himself from Thomas Nelson Page, who he claimed was "disguising the harshness of slavery under the mask of sentiment" ("Post-Bellum" 193). But racial difference is highlighted by dialect in Chesnutt's stories just as it is in Page's writing. Chesnutt even abandoned the dialect tales for a while but returned under pressure from his editor.

Chesnutt does not seem to relish the dialect for the sound itself, as I argued with Harris, but uses it in order to put the content of Uncle Julius's stories with their strong indictment of slavery in Julius's own voice. In "Po' Sandy," for example, when Julius reaches the climactic end to his tragic story of Sandy's death, he extends the reach of the story to the present moment and beyond: "En folks sez dat de ole school'ouse, er any yuther house s'at got any er dat lumber in it w'at wuz sawed out'n de tree w'at Sandy wuz turnt inter, is gwine ter be ha'nted tel de las' piece er plank is rotted en crumble' inter dus'" (*Conjure Tales* 60). The dialect keeps the attention on Julius telling the story and keeps the reader closer to the African American oral tradition that Chesnutt portrays: "En folks sez" (60). The African American body haunting the very lumber of the house should certainly be made present in Julius's voice. When Gavin Jones argues that "dialect could encode the possibility of resistance," he points to the importance of "recording the subversive voices in which alternate versions of reality were engendered" (11). Eric Sundquist, in analyzing the larger cultural conversation at the time about whether African American writers should use dialect, discusses Chesnutt's choice in the context of his contemporaries such as Paul Lawrence Dunbar and James Weldon Johnson. Sundquist argues that Chesnutt along with Du Bois "waged the battle for African American cultural integrity" by "making their own literary acts not distinct from but continuous with the unwritten, signifying 'word-shadows' of the black spirituals and black folktales" (*To Wake* 305). Uncle Julius in the end worries the reader less than Uncle Remus because he is able to gain an equal footing with John despite the difference in language—or perhaps because of that very difference. The dialect reminds the reader that the speakers are not simply characters in a written story but take on the power of storytellers in oral tradition.

***

In examining the genre of the frame tale from its beginnings in India three millennia ago to its inception in medieval times, Bonnie Irwin finds that the form emphasizes not just orality but the ability of the oral storyteller: "While holding the floor, the narrator is the most powerful figure in the performance context. Thus a lowly miller, providing he is a skilled storyteller, can exert the same power over Chaucer's pilgrims as does the noble knight. Whoever is narrating dominates the social hierarchy of the performance event, regardless of his or her station in any other context" (49). When Remus and Julius tell their tales, they have the power of the oral storyteller to construct worlds in language; even when Remus is passing down known stories, he has the power to shape the stories to his pleasing. In oral tradition it is not the stories themselves that matter as much as how they are told; the focus is on the teller. Once the reader can see Remus and Julius as not just characters in written books but as representative oral storytellers, their power becomes clear.

Critics have certainly not seen Uncle Remus as a powerful figure. The common complaint is that as a "happy darky" Remus gives us a picture of slavery that is harmless and nostalgic. Joel Chandler Harris actually seems to point critics in this direction in his introduction when he describes Remus as a former slave "who has nothing but pleasant memories of the discipline of slavery" (47). Harris's comment, however, is a bit more complicated than this one phrase and is framed itself as part of a larger conjecture that begins, "If the reader not familiar with plantation life will imagine that the myth-stories of Uncle Remus . . ." (46). The reader is in an abstract world before ever getting to Remus himself, and that abstract world could be interpreted in a number of ways. However, I cannot help but hear some humor in Harris's introduction. If the introduction is the frame of the entire collection and Harris is the narrator of this frame, he would certainly be in the tradition of the humorist to tell the reader not to pay attention to the important things and to see the stories as simply stories. Mark Twain tells his reader in his notice to _Huckleberry Finn_, "Persons attempting to find a motive in this narrative will be prosecuted; persons attempting to find a moral in it will be banished; persons attempting to find a plot in it will be shot" (xxix). Regardless of whether the author can be taken at face value, the question of whether Remus is a product of plantation myth, and thereby rendered impotent, can also be answered by looking at the actual frame tales. Critics who dismiss Remus see him as situated strictly in the frame and thus a product of Harris's written product, too separate from the African folktales to be interesting. Dianne Armstrong, for example, argues that because Remus "serves as a wedge between readers' imminent confrontation with the stories' full impact (filtered again through the child), and their conceivable aversion to the more unpleasant aspects, he obstructs the processing of political awareness" (73). Here not only is Remus powerless, he negates the power of the "tales' sinister thrust" and gives the reader a cushion (Armstrong 73). The reader can ignore the tales because the reader, like the boy, has the harmless counterexample of Remus ever present. One exception to this critical consensus is Jefferson Humphries, who finds Remus's power through his storytelling: "The old black man, though he does not subject the white audience to humiliation, certainly does manipulate, 'deceive' him—deception and verbal manipulation being the very essence of successful storytelling" (182). I will, of course, agree that Remus has power as a storyteller, but the powers of manipulation and deception that Humphries finds seem unnecessarily negative. I will read Remus's power as that to convince, to connect, to make the audience see the world as he sees it.

Remus's tells stories of his own world, though the reader must see through the animal tales to understand how they are showing Remus's world. One way of connecting the tales to Uncle Remus is to see the tales as allegory with Brer Rabbit, the weak but clever animal standing in for the African slave, who is oppressed but can use his smarts to negotiate a system in which he has no power. Joel Chandler Harris himself again points in this direction in his introduction, when he suggests the stories may be allegorical because "it needs no scientific investigation to show why he selects as his hero the weakest and most harmless of all animals, and brings him out victorious in contests with the bear, the wolf, and the fox. It is not virtue that triumphs, but helplessness; it is not malice, but mischievousness" (44). The first and most well-known story of the collection proves a good example. Brer Rabbit has fallen for Brer Fox's trick and gotten so stuck in the tar baby he is helpless to fight the fox or to run away. Brer Fox, having all the power, then deliberates on the best way to kill the rabbit. Brer Rabbit then infamously begs to be killed by any means except by being flung in the brier patch. Brer Fox, wanting to inflict as much pain as possible, decides on the method the rabbit seems to fear the most and flings him in the brier patch. This is exactly, of course, what the rabbit wants; he is not hurt but escapes because he was "bred en bawn in a brier-patch" (64). A rabbit is physically no match for a fox, but the Brer Rabbit of Remus's tales can outsmart the fox and thus level the playing field.

While reading the tales allegorically makes their telling by Remus understandable, the allegory is not as simple as saying Brer Rabbit is a slave and the fox, the wolf, and the bear are white slave owners. The rabbit does not always win; his pride sometimes gets in the way of his good sense. He, for example, loses his tail in one story because he listens to Brer Fox and sticks the tail in a stream all night to gather fish. Brer Rabbit is also not unique in using his wits to outsmart the other animals. Brer Fox initially tricks him by fashioning the tar baby, and Brer Tarrypin tricks him in a race by using several members of his family to tag team and beat the rabbit to the finish line. So it is not the case of the weak character tricking the strong character; all the animals are trying to outtrick each other. The other animals seem to stand in for slaves at times as well. In the story "Old Mr. Rabbit, He's a Good Fisherman" the reader is told that Brer Rabbit, Brer Fox, Brer Coon, and Brer B'ar are all working in the fields clearing new ground. Lucinda MacKethan points out that the character of Mr. Man seems most representative of the white slave owners as he "represents an intrusion of the white master's influence into the dream from which the Negro legends are constructed. He is the only figure whose superiority is granted automatically, and he is the only one who is shown using the other creatures to do his labor for him" (71).

Even if, however, the animals are all allegorically slaves and Mr. Man is white power, his presence is so negligible that the allegory of the weak conquering the strong is weightless. The tales and their characters, then, do not neatly line up in allegorical terms.

The tales are also more complex than their depiction of animals suggests. Paula Connolly argues that the use of animals to make the tales seem "childish" was a strategy to protect the storytellers: "Slaves were able to recount them in public without fear of retribution. Indeed, that categorization of adult men and women as 'childlike' creatures who needed the protection of whites served as a rationalization for slavery itself" (153). While Connolly is certainly correct about the protection gained by coding critiques of slavery into seemingly harmless forms, I think there is yet another way to read Remus's use of animal tales to tell his story.[7] Tales that involve animals could point to a more complicated reading in that the tales discuss the natural order of the world. Remus cannot openly discuss power structures and subversion using black and white characters; by discussing animals, the stories delve into societal issues that are presented as simply part of earthly existence. When telling the story of the deluge, Remus sets the time of the story "way back yander, 'fo' you wuz borned, honey, en 'fo' Mars John er Miss Sally wuz borned—way back yander 'fo' enny un us wuz borned" (64). In this time before people, Remus first asserts that animals "had lots mo' sense" but then says that "dey had sense same like folks" (64). The animals here are both standing in for people and standing for original society, what is inherent in "folks" now. When the little boy protests that Brer Tarrypin cheated when he won the race against the rabbit, Remus responds, "Co'se honey. De beastesses 'gun ter cheat, en den fokes tuck it up, en hit keep on spreadin'" (105). By telling tales about the earth's first creatures, the animals, Remus suggests that he is simply portraying how the world works.

Remus's stories also display Remus's values. In this world might does not make right; trickery is the name of the game with the only goal being survival. When the little boy is concerned that Brer Possum's death is not fair because he did not steal the butter, Remus answers, "In dis worril, lots er fokes is gotter suffer fer udder fokes sins" (102). Although his answer seems to suggest that the animal tales share the same values as "dis worril," the rabbit is victorious in Remus's stories not because he is the typical hero of Western literature full of courage and virtue but frankly because he can lie better than the other animals. He is the archetypal trickster figure, who undermines systems and structures by lying, cheating, and stealing. He plays on the other characters' weaknesses and sympathies with no sign of remorse. Brer Rabbit, for example, tricks Brer B'ar into sticking his head into a hol-

low tree to look for honey and causes his death by stirring up the bees. Although Remus remarks that the way the Rabbit did it "wuz sinful," there is
not an expression of guilt in the story (136). Remus's Brer Rabbit portrays
the viewpoint of someone outside the system, invested only in figuring out
how to overthrow those in power. While it might make sense, as Harris suggests, that the stories glory in the weak character triumphing over the strong,
the methods used and thus valued also point to the narrator, Uncle Remus,
and his choice of stories.

To be fair, though, Harris and his fictional narrator Uncle Remus borrow
the Brer Rabbit stories from oral tradition. Remus is not depicted as creating these tales of trickery but merely repeating them. However, the stories are
his personally and not just his as a representative slave. How he shapes them
is the key, as it always is in oral tradition; the emphasis is not on what the
story is but how it is told. From the very beginning, in "Uncle Remus Initi-
ates the Little Boy," the reader knows that the rabbit will always come out if
not the winner then at least a survivor: "En Brer Fox ain't never kotch 'im
yet, en w'at's mo', honey, he ain't gwineter" (57). The plot is then not the
key concern, but rather how that rabbit gets away and thus how Remus spins
the tale. The tales themselves have antecedents back to Africa, but clues exist
throughout, in the form of references to Remus's American world, that he is
taking the tales and shaping them to make them his own. At least twice the
tales refer to "patter-rollers," which Harris footnotes and explains, "Patrols.
In the country districts, order was kept on the plantations at night by the
knowledge that they were liable to be visited at any moment by the patrols"
(71). The tales are changed to include aspects of American slavery. Remus
also includes his own experience. In the story of the deluge when he discusses the animals gathering and debating various issues, he compares them
to the little boy's father: "Dey spoke speeches, en hollered, en cusst, en flung
der langwidge 'roun' des like w'en yo' daddy waz gwineter run fer de legislater
en got lef" (65). His description of the animals' meeting becomes a parody
of the legislative process with the crawfish getting trampled by the elephants
and unable to get attention over all the clamor. Remus also shapes the stories by his selection; he picks the story that fits his particular context. When
he is mad at the little boy for telling on his little brother, he tells the story of
Jack Sparrer, a tattletale who gets eaten by the Brer Fox. Remus often deflects
his power by referring to the authority of the tale itself, as when the little boy
asks who Miss Meadows was and Remus simply responds, "She wuz in de
tale, Miss Meadows en de gals wuz, en de tale I give you like hi't wer' gun ter
me" (67). But this deflection reflects less a lack of authority on Remus's part
than the storyteller's trick of leading his audience on. When, for example,

Brer Rabbit is stuck on the tar baby and the little boy asks if the fox eats the rabbit, Remus first responds, "Dat's all de fur de tale goes," but then gives some possibilities, "Some say Jedge B'ar come 'long en loosed 'im—some say he didn't" (59). Later, of course, Remus tells the "rest" of the tale, which just so happens not to fit either of the former versions. The tales, then, can be manipulated and shaped, by none other than the storyteller, Remus.

Uncle Julius in Charles Chesnutt's *The Conjure Woman* gains even more power through his role as narrator. Many critics see his power evidenced in the tangible objects he obtains by telling stories to the northern couple, John and Annie.[8] When Julius first meets them, he tries to dissuade John from buying the vineyard by telling him it was "goophered." At the end of the story John objects to the conclusion that the vineyard is worthless by asserting that some of the vines are alive and obviously bearing fruit, since Julius is eating a hat full of grapes when John and Annie meet him. Julius is quick to answer that "dey did 'pear ter die, but a few un 'em come out ag'in, en is mixed in 'mongs' de yuthers. I ain' skeered ter eat de grapes 'caze I knows de old vimes fum do noo ones; but wid strangers dey ain' no tellin' w'at mought happen" (*Conjure Tales* 33–34). John later discovers that Julius had been deriving a "respectable revenue from the product of the neglected grapevines" and guesses this is why Julius was advising him against buying the land. Julius, however, does successfully sell his expertise, and John hires him. With almost every story from this point forward, Julius manages to gain something through its telling. When he convinces Annie that the lumber from the schoolhouse is haunted, he is able to use the schoolhouse for his church meetings. When he tells the story of Mars Jeems being turned into a slave, he is able to negotiate the rehiring of his grandson. He convinces John to buy a horse, which he may have some stake in, by telling a story about a man turned into a mule. He thus gains power through his storytelling by influencing John's and Annie's decisions. Even John begins to see the effect of the stories and discusses in his ending frames what might have motivated Julius to tell each tale. With the purchase of what ends up being a poor horse, John can only speculate that Julius benefited financially by remarking that Julius has new clothes with no apparent means of purchasing them. John's rather sarcastic remarks reduce Julius to simply a con man, and a relatively poor one since John can so easily see through Julius's schemes. Julius is dependent on John, so even in his manipulation of John's and Annie's choices for his gain, the choices themselves, from buying land to building a kitchen, are still not his.

Where Julius's power truly lies is thus not in the accumulation of things; he in fact depicts gain and greed as the motivation for much suffering in slavery. The power is in his ability to tell the story of the people he knew and the atrocities of the slave system. Slaves are portrayed solely commodities, such as when Mars Dugal buys and sells Henry as the slave's condition improves and worsens with the goophered grapevines and when Becky is traded for a prize racehorse because her master did not have the money to buy the horse outright. The separation of families routinely enacted in slavery is in just about every story. Tenie, for example, uses conjure to turn her husband, Sandy, into a tree to prevent their separation, and Becky's baby is taken away from her. The underlying violence of the slave system is revealed when Mars Jeems, transformed into the new slave, is repeatedly beaten and starved by an eager overseer and Sandy is sawed into lumber while Tenie has to watch, mirroring the reality of slavery when slaves had to watch helplessly as brutality was inflicted on their family members. In an attempt to soften the blow of Julius's portrayal of slavery, John attributes the stories to Julius's desire for gain. Julius is telling the truth of slavery, something Frederick Douglass explains that slaves themselves were forbidden to do. In discussing the economics of Julius's storytelling, Richard Brodhead points out that although Julius gains things by his stories, he also "must be giving something in return" in that "he is giving up his people's life as other people's entertainment. Like a long line of black show business successes in American white culture he wins an enhanced social place for himself by making African-American expressive forms and 'soul' available to others' imaginative participation and consumption" (Introduction 12). Brodhead can use the word "entertainment" because of the multiple times John and Annie request Julius to tell a story to relieve their boredom, but entertainment does not fully describe what John and Annie receive in the stories. With the harsh truth of slavery Julius is able to tell, he is more educator than entertainer. His power comes in revealing the effects of exploitation.[9]

Even without identifying Julius's economic motives, John can still dismiss the stories' power on the basis that they use supernatural elements and are thus, of course, not true. Annie responds to the story of Tenie and Sandy by exclaiming, "What a system it was, under which such things were possible!" (60). Annie has paid attention to the underlying problem of the separation of families and the torture of watching a loved one killed, but John responds, "Are you seriously considering the possibility of a man's being turned into a tree?" (60). John can dismiss the "absurdly impossible yarn" because the plot is based on the ability of conjure to turn people into things, but he also dismisses, along with the magic, the critique of slavery. In the portrayal of John, Chesnutt seems to acknowledge the effect of his inclusion of the supernatural to his message about slavery. In his essay "Superstitions and Folk-

Lore of the South," Chesnutt indeed distances himself from the irrational belief and practice, finding it a "mere lack of enlightenment" and "relics of ancestral barbarism" (232). Chesnutt's superior and rational tone in the essay actually places him very close to John in point of view. So the obvious question is: if the inclusion of supernatural elements would diminish the power of the stories, why include them?

The goopher element mixed into every single story in the collection cannot be eliminated because it plays an essential role: it shows the retention of African culture. Just as Julius must speak of slavery's atrocities in his own voice with his own dialect, the tales must be told through African culture if Julius is to assert some power. Goopher or conjure is an African cultural practice that survived the Middle Passage to America and is set up as distinct from Western Christian belief. When Tenie, for example, tells Sandy that she is a "cunjuh 'oman," she explains that she had not practiced in fifteen years because "I got religion" (45). In "The Conjurer's Revenge" the conjure man decides to change Primus back to a man before he dies because he has been converted at a camp meeting. He says, "I's be'n a monst'us sinner man, en I's done a power er wickedness endyoin' er my days; but de good Lawd is wash' my sins erway, en I feels now dat I's boun' fer de kingdom" (122–23). The practice of conjure is African and the slaves' alone. Conjure is then a key element in the stories because it gives the slaves power. Aunt Peggy is able to arrange for Becky to be bought back so she can be with her baby, to turn Hannibal into a lunatic so Chloe can be with Jeff, and to give Dan a life-charm so no one can harm him. Her power is even acknowledged by the white community when Mars Dugal hires her to goopher his grapevines. Moreover, Aunt Peggy has the power to conjure white people, as she does when Mars Jeems turns into a slave for a few days. Goopher is then central to the power of the stories.

Although Chesnutt seems to distance himself from conjure in his essay, his response may actually be a bit more complicated. Chesnutt acknowledges that elements of the stories he thought he had made up were "but dormant ideas, lodged in my childish mind by old Aunt This and old Uncle That, and awaiting only the spur of imagination to bring them again to the surface" ("Superstitions" 232). Chesnutt places his use of conjure firmly within an African American tradition; Chesnutt also identifies that tradition as oral storytelling. By preserving conjure in his stories of slavery, Chesnutt keeps a powerful symbol of African culture and allows Uncle Julius to tell his own stories, those of the truth of slavery, his own way, by passing down African oral tradition.

By depicting Uncle Remus and Uncle Julius as telling their own stories in their own voices, Harris and Chesnutt portray characters who are powerful storytellers. Their use of the frame tale, however, also depicts the audiences for the tales. In oral tradition the audience is, of course, flesh and blood, immediate, and concrete. Chesnutt and Harris try to imitate this live audience by portraying characters listening to the tales. Listeners for oral storytelling have the ability to interrupt, to ask questions, to modify a tale, and ultimately to retell the story and become storytellers themselves. The frame tales play with this interchange between teller and listener by giving the illusion of active listeners for these powerful storytellers.

This interchange thus is completely missed if we separate the tale from the frame in Harris's work, and the separation then diminishes the power of the storyteller; without an audience, the story is a tree falling in the forest with no witnesses, sound waves but no sound. Critics who argue for the separation of frame from tale want to preserve the African American tradition of the Brer Rabbit stories but wash them clean of the racist frame produced by Harris. Robert Bone uses the image of the kernel and the husk; the kernel was not "tampered with," not, that is, tainted by the "external wrappings" (23). Dianne Armstrong and Paula Connolly locate the separation in the text itself, as the tales, in Connolly's words, "*fight* the frame of happy Uncle Remus and the concurrent idyllic presentation of slavery" (152). The critics' motives are understandable; the way Uncle Remus panders to the child and seems overly delighted by small gifts of food in the framing narratives makes the reader wince, but separating out the stories from their context causes the reader to lose the oral storytelling at their core.

Uncle Remus is not just telling stories to the big, wide world, as an author of a written text might address an unknown audience or an anonymous "reader." He is telling the tales *to* the "little boy," a young white boy whose very presence is felt not just in the frames but throughout the stories themselves. Many of the stories are in fact prompted by the little boy asking Remus a question. The boy, for example, hears how the rabbit got out of his mess with the tar baby by asking, "Did the fox kill and eat the rabbit when he caught him with the Tar-Baby?" (62). The boy's questions also appear within many stories. He interrupts to ask for clarifications, such as the meaning of "swaje yo' bag" in reference to the rabbit taking Miss Cow's milk, or for further information, as when he asks Remus, "Did you ever see a witch?" (143). The questions highlight his presence as the "live" audience for the stories.

The boy also reacts to the stories. For example, after the story of the deluge, he asks Remus where the ark was and complains when Remus begins to tell a story about Brer Wolf after Remus had told of the wolf's death in a previous story. The reactions provide the interchange central to oral storytelling.

We still should examine why Harris chose as his audience a little boy. One potential problem with the choice is that it diminishes the power of Remus, an elderly man, to have to tell his stories to a child instead of to his peers. The problem is similar to that of Twain's use of Huckleberry Finn to help and befriend Jim. Huck makes the revolutionary acknowledgment that Jim is his equal, but this lovely relationship is between an adult black man and a young white boy.[10] A second problem is that by using a white boy, the tales are taken out of their primary social context. Julius Lester argues that while the use of the white boy "added to the appeal and accessibility of the tales for whites, it leaves the reader with no sense of the important roles the tales played in black life. The telling of black folktales, and indeed tales of all cultures, was a social event bringing together adults and children" (*Tales* xv). Alice Walker writes a harsh critique of Harris by explaining her childhood reaction to the Walt Disney movie based on Harris's stories. Her central complaint is the choice of white children for the audience: "Uncle Remus in the movie saw fit largely to ignore his own children and grandchildren in order to pass on our heritage—indeed, our birthright—to patronizing white children, who seemed to regard him as a kind of talking teddy bear" (31). One simple explanation of Harris's choice is that this is how he first heard the tales himself. At thirteen Harris worked on the Turner plantation, and he befriended two slaves, Uncle George Tarrell and Old Harbert, who told stories at night to the Turner children and to Harris (Bickley 23).

Despite the obvious problems with the choice of audience, this choice is important because the little boy plays the part of the outsider in oral storytelling. In the humor tradition Harris borrows from, the audience is often an outsider, who does not at first understand the context and implications of the story. One can tell, for example, a tall tale about a local person or custom only to a stranger who does not know better. Insiders or "locals" may also participate, but they already know the punch lines. Henry Wonham in his study of the tall tale explains that the form distinguishes between insiders who know the joke and outsiders who either accept the story at face value or flatly deny it instead of playing along, making the oral storytelling into a "game of initiation and exclusion" (28). The humor that these stories as well as those of Harris deploy is the humor Henri Bergson in his influential essay "Laughter" describes as a social phenomenon. Bergson discusses the laughter that "appears to stand in need of an echo" (64). Humor can draw the line between insiders and outsiders; those who are in the group get the jokes. In Bergson's words, humor "implies a kind of freemansonry, or even complicity, with other laughers, real or imaginary" (64). Oral storytelling, which is inherently social, becomes a way of building a group.

To be sure, Remus's stories of the wily rabbit outsmarting stronger but rather slow-witted animals are not humorous in a lighthearted way. Harris himself warns that the humor has a serious side in his introduction: "I am advised by my publishers that this book is to be included in their catalogue of humorous publications, and this friendly warning gives me an opportunity to say that however humorous it may be in effect, its intention is perfectly serious; and, even if it were otherwise, it seems to me that a volume written wholly in dialect must have its solemn, not to say melancholy, features" (39). When, for example, Brer Rabbit tells Brer Wolf he is only "tellin' my chilluns w'at a nice man you is," while he boils water he will later use to scald the wolf to death, the rabbit's children "had ter put der han's on der mouf fer ter keep fun laffin'" (91–92). The children see the humor, but the wolf does not yet get the joke. The concept of humor here is social and serious.

The question is whether the little boy can be an insider to this dark humor. Although the little boy's ancestors were slave owners, he is not yet fully immersed in his own social context, much less the African-influenced world of Remus's stories with their values of trickery and deceit. There are a few hints, though admittedly subtle, that the boy is catching on. When he brings Uncle Remus a pie, Remus wonders aloud if the boy stole the cupboard key to get it; the boy answers, "Well, I saw the pie lying there, Uncle Remus, and I just thought I'd fetch it out to you" (84). When Remus tells the story of the plantation witch, the little boy hesitates at first to believe him because "Papa says there ain't any witches" (144). But under the spell of Remus's story, he later asks, "Do they get out of their skins?" (145). The reader is left, however, with only these few hints that the boy might be catching on to the content of the stories. John Callahan argues that Harris "elevates culture above politics" in not showing the stories in a context that could produce the "politics of radical change" (38). Harris's choice, however, may be even more radical. Remus tells stories depicting the overthrow of power to the next inheritor of the system of white patriarchy. The frame then matches the subversive nature of the tales. The oral storytelling manages to form at least fictionally a mixed community. Unfortunately this community is only theoretical. Whatever Harris's intentions, readers of *Uncle Remus: His Songs and His Sayings* and certainly viewers of the Walt Disney movie did not see the dark humor of the tales. As Lyle Glazier argues, readers "loved Miss Sally, Mars Jeems, Old Miss, John Huntindon, and the small boy. Most of all they loved Uncle

Remus, such a lovable, comforting, kind old Darkey, who makes things all right for everybody's conscience" (73). Chesnutt, however, is able to take this theoretical possibility of a mixed audience from Harris's work and bring it closer to life in his depiction of John and Annie.

Chesnutt gives Uncle Julius an audience of his peers, a northern white couple who move south for health reasons and to profit from post–Civil War conditions. Because they are from the North, they play the role the little boy does for Remus, as outsiders in need of education. Through Julius's stories they learn about the land they bought, its former inhabitants, their neighbors, and the history of the slaves who lived in the area. That Julius keeps his audience in mind is evident in how appropriate each story is to the current situation narrated in the frame. That John and Annie act the part of the live audience in oral storytelling is evident in their questions and reactions, which connect frame to story, audience to storyteller.

The interchange between Julius and his audience is more pronounced than in Harris's work because John and Annie are adults and can respond to Julius's story as peers. The stories themselves are prompted, as they are in Harris's work, by the audience. Annie and John often ask questions that lead to Julius telling a story. When they first meet Julius and he tries to dissuade them from purchasing the land by explaining that it is goophered, John asks, "How do you know it is bewitched?" (*Conjure Tales* 12). Later when the three witness a neighbor, Mr. McLean, beating his horse and Julius mentions the nightmare the young man's grandfather had, John asks, "What was it about Mr. McLean's dream, Julius?" (70). Other stories are prompted by the audience outright asking for them. When Julius mentions the gray wolf's haunt, John says, "Tell us about it, Uncle Julius. . . . A story will be a godsend today" (167). John again asks Julius to "tell us the tale" when Julius explains the horse will not cross the branch because she remembers Chloe (203). The questions and requests show a willing and receptive audience. John and Annie may not always understand or sympathize with Julius's stories, but they are at least willing to listen to them.

Their reactions to the stories are in fact mixed. Often the discussion in the ending frame is about the truth of the story. After Julius tells the first tale of the goophered grapevine, Annie responds, "Is that story true?" (33). After "Mars Jeems's Nightmare," both Annie and John question its validity. Annie first calls the story "strange," and then suggests that "Solomon's explanation is quite improbable" (100). John sarcastically asks, "By the way, did you make that up all by yourself?" (101). His question points to his disbelief that the events of the story actually happened, but Julius responds to the last part of his question, "by yourself," by assuring John "I heard dat tale befo' you er Mis' Annie dere wuz bawn, suh" (101). His answer deflects the question of truth by positing the tale back into oral tradition where the content of tales is handed down from one teller to the next. Besides the discussions of the stories' truthfulness, the most dramatic reaction to a story occurs after the telling of "Hot-Foot Hannibal." Annie's sister Mabel reunites with her fiancé Malcolm Murchison, although she had sworn that she never wanted to see him again. All of the reactions highlight Chesnutt's attempt to portray the stories as oral and as being told to an audience.

John and Annie as the outsider audience do not always understand the tales; they do not, especially at first, get the jokes. The humor is even darker than in the Uncle Remus stories and usually comes in the form of cruel irony. Dan is tricked by the conjurer into killing his own wife, for example, and another conjure man dies before completely turning Primus back into a human, leaving him with a mule's foot. Glenda Carpio aptly describes the difficult dynamics of Chesnutt's humor: "The different levels of irony that Chesnutt creates through the structure of his tales and the comic aspects on which he relies—many of which engage with the racist images and ideologies of American popular culture—are often in conflict with the laughter that the stories represent, a laughter that, at its most powerful, suggests the violence and pain of slavery" (37).

Getting the jokes in Chesnutt's stories, then, may mean becoming one of the insiders, but what that ticket buys is a knowledge of devastation. The model for a white audience getting the joke may actually be given in one of the stories, "Mars Jeems Nightmare." Solomon, a slave on Mars Jeems's plantation, is separated from his "junesey," so he asks Aunt Peggy to create a goopher to make Mars Jeems treat his slaves better. Aunt Peggy creates a powder for the cook to put in Mars Jeems's food to cause him to have a nightmare. When Mars Jeems goes away on business, his overseer Nick Johnson takes over and inflicts much pain and hardship on all the slaves, but especially a new slave who seems not to know how to work or behave as a slave. One day Solomon discovers Mars Jeems in the woods in ragged clothes and guesses that Aunt Peggy turned him temporarily into a slave. Mars Jeems certainly behaves differently after this point, working his slaves less and letting them get married. The sign, however, that Mars Jeems gets it, that is understands what it means to be a slave, is laughter. When he arrives back at his plantation, he asks Nick all about the new slave. As Nick tells the story of how inept the slave was and how harsh Nick was in return, Mars Jeems "lafft en lafft, 'tel it 'peared lack he wuz des gwine ter bu'st" (*Conjure Tales* 95). Mars Jeems has become an insider and now gets the joke. He understands that the overseer is cruel and untrustworthy. Only a reader of the story may be able to appreciate the irony of that humor, however. Carpio points out that "as a result of Jeems's transformation, his slaves are much more productive, producing capital gain. A master's moral edification thus results not in the end of slavery but in its perfection" (60). Solomon's situation as a slave may have improved when his master laughs, but the slave system remains intact.

Of the two fictional listeners, Annie is the first to understand the stories' larger ideas because she reacts emotionally to the characters and does not, as John does, weigh the probability of the events or try to determine Julius's economic motive. She responds to "Po' Sandy" by feeling sorry for Tenie, while John disputes the notion that a man can be turned into a tree. When Annie tells John that she does not want to use the lumber from the schoolhouse to build her new kitchen, he responds, "You wouldn't for a moment allow yourself . . . to be influenced by that absurdly impossible yarn which Julius was spinning to-day?" (61). Annie admits the story is "absurd," but explains that she would not "be able to take any pleasure in that kitchen it if were built out of that lumber" (61). The story not only relates the pathetic situation of Tenie having to watch as her husband is killed but also speaks to the larger economics of slavery, where the slaves did not profit from their own labor. The schoolhouse might belong to John and Annie legally, but in spirit it belongs to the people, such as Julius, who worked the land. Annie gets the message, and realizes that she would not find "pleasure" at the expense of another person. The humor comes when Annie grants permission to Julius to use the schoolhouse for his church. John wants to know what they will do with the ghost, and Annie replies, "Uncle Julius says that ghosts never disturb religious worship, but that if Sandy's spirit *should* happen to stray into meeting by mistake, no doubt the preaching would do it good" (63). Slavery's ghosts are not going to haunt African Americans; if Sandy's ghost finds a church meeting conducted by African Americans in their own building, the worship might indeed "do it good."

That Annie is getting the joke is evidenced in the frame of "Sis' Becky's Pickaninny," when Annie is able to provide the punch line. Julius tells the story to support his carrying a rabbit's foot around for luck. After Julius tells the story of Becky's separation and then reuniting with her baby, John responds, "That is a very ingenious fairy tale." Annie replies, "Why, John! the story bears the stamp of truth, if ever a story did." The ever-rational John questions the elements of conjure in the story, but Annie responds that they are "mere ornamental details and not at all essential" (159). When John then tries to point out that the story does not prove that a rabbit's foot brings good luck, Julius allows Annie to explain the point: "I rather suspect that

Sis' Becky had no rabbit's foot" (160). Annie is correct, as Julius claims she "hit de bull's-eye de fus'fire" (160). Annie understands the story well enough to see past its use of conjure to the underlying truth about the situation of families in slavery. Becky does not have the power to keep her family intact and so must rely on conjure or just plain luck. Luck is the answer of a people without agency. Paul Petrie suggests that Annie is able to understand the tales better than John because the stories need a sympathetic ear; Chesnutt then finds one potential audience in the "cadre of white, women readers steeped in the conventions of sentimental romance and its undergirding moral philosophy" (192-93). Although John does not respond as well as Annie and distances himself through rationality, his willingness to listen to the stories, his requests for the stories, and his overall understanding that Julius's stories reveal the tragic dimensions of slavery show that he begins to understand at least fractionally the tragedy of slavery even if he is not able to become the ideal audience Annie is.

Chesnutt's depiction of John and Annie brings the reader closer to that ideal of a community created through storytelling. Chesnutt attempts to find a fictional space where Julius as storyteller can reach John and Annie as an audience. William Gleason discusses the space of the piazza where Julius usually tells his stories as a middle ground between the house and the land, between white and black. The space, however, is as fictional as John and Annie. Chesnutt mimics the dynamics of oral storytelling in his frame tales by depicting characters as listeners, but these characters are still bound by the written page; they are not flesh and blood. It is telling, however, to see what Chesnutt imagines when giving his storyteller Julius an audience. He imagines two white people who not only listen to Julius's tales but, at least in Annie's case, understand their underlying message. He is hoping for an audience to get the joke.

***

When the audience gets the joke, they become part of the inside group; in racial terms in these two works that means the white audience must become black. Harris and Chesnutt do not, however, align themselves with the minstrel tradition of putting on whiteness or blackness by painting a face. The mixing here is more a matter of recognizing sameness, becoming community, and laughing together at the humor of fallible humans trying to assert power. The ability for the audience to change races is implied in both texts by various transformations. In Chesnutt's text the conjure element allows for the possibility of a person to become a different kind of being. Sandy becomes a tree, Primus becomes a mule, Becky's baby becomes first a hummingbird then a mockingbird, Dan becomes a wolf, and Henry becomes a grapevine. Uncle Remus's stories do not include conjure, so the changes are not as bold, but the ability to become something else is still evident. When Brer Tarrypin wins the race, he does so by placing his family members along the route so that when Brer Rabbit calls toward the wooded route the tarrypin picks, someone crawls out and answers back. All of the tarrypins have become Brer Tarrypin. In another story when Brer Fox finds Brer Rabbit's children home alone, a bird's voice gives them various instructions to avoid getting caught by the fox. Brer Rabbit arrives home at the end, but it is clear that he was the voice of the bird in the story. In one story, however, the metamorphosis is as blatant as those in Uncle Julius's stories of conjure. In the story of the plantation witch, Remus explains to the little boy that witches can take off their skin and become other creatures, from owls to cats. The ability to change is set up in each text through these transformations, but both writers push a bit further in experimenting with racial mixing by suggesting that people can indeed change race.

Harris and Chesnutt must be careful, of course, in doing this not to go too far and offend their audiences. Chesnutt wraps his experiment in the conjure that John is so quick to dismiss, perhaps to soften the force of the story. In "Mars Jeems's Nightmare" the slave owner Mars Jeems is by all accounts a bad master; even his intended fiancée refuses to marry him when she hears how he treats his slaves. The breaking point for the slave Solomon is when Mars Jeems sends away the woman he loves simply because Jeems does not allow his slaves "sech foolishness" (74). Aunt Peggy agrees to intervene and conjure the master but admits she "has ter be kinder keeful 'bout cunj'in' w'ite folks" (77). When Mars Jeems leaves town for a few days, Solomon forgets about the conjure, focusing his attention on Nick Johnson, the overseer, and his interactions with a new slave. The new slave does not know how to speak correctly to the overseer or how to work and ends up getting whipped and starved until Nick gives up and sends him back. Solomon does not figure out that the new slave is Mars Jeems transformed into a black man until Aunt Peggy warns him that he must give the new slave a special sweet potato to eat before he is shipped out of town. Solomon finds his old master in the woods in tattered clothes; Mars Jeems thinks he has just had a "monst'us bad dream," but Solomon suspects that Mars Jeems was temporarily changed from white to black (91). Although John and Annie question Solomon's interpretation of the events, his name alludes to the biblical Solomon, whose gift was wisdom. By portraying the transformation as at best a dream and at worst a product of conjure, Chesnutt keeps his racial mixing in purely fictional territory. Chesnutt does not end the story with Jeems acknowledging the full humanity of his slaves and freeing them. The union is not between races but shifts to marriage, as Jeems allows Solomon to reunite with his woman and Jeems's changed behavior convinces his former fiancée to marry him. Although carefully wrapped in various fictional discourses, the possibility for a white person to become black and for the races thus to mix is certainly present.

Harris approaches the possibility late in his collection in the story "Why the Negro Is Black," one of the few stories that is not an animal tale. The story is occasioned by the little boy noticing Remus's hands are white, a fact that is "such a source of wonder" that he asks Remus about it. Remus first tells him that "dey wuz a time w'en all de w'ite folks 'uz black—blacker dan me" (150). The little boy laughs because he thinks that Uncle Remus is tricking him, but Remus remains serious and answers, "Niggers is niggers now, but de time wuz w'en we 'uz all niggers tergedder" (151). He then tells a story of a time when all people were black. Someone discovered a pond that would wash the skin white. The people who got to the pond first came out very white, those that followed only got enough water to make them mulatto, and when the last ones came, there was just enough water to "paddle about wid der foots en dabble in it wid der han's" (151). On the surface, Remus's story seems harmless and aligned to the minstrel tradition; he depicts black people as simply ignorant and whiteness as cleansing and preferred. The story, however, also suggests the possibility of racial mixture, of white being black and black becoming white.

The two authors themselves seem to embody the racial mixing they write into their story collections. Charles Chesnutt explains that when he first published *The Conjure Woman* his race "was never mentioned by the publishers in announcing or advertising the book." At the time, he suggests, it was not important: "From my own viewpoint it was a personal matter. It never occurred to me to claim any merit because of it, and I have always resented the denial of anything on account of it." When news of Chesnutt's race surfaced, he wryly notes that one critic claimed disbelief: "this is obviously untrue, because no Negro could possibly have written these books" ("Post-Bellum" 194). Settling that question is certainly a more subtle matter for Chesnutt than sheer ability. His light skin made it difficult for him growing up to fit in with either white or black societies. J. Noel Heermance reports in his biography on Chesnutt that at age twenty-three Chesnutt wrote in his diary that he was "neither fish, flesh, nor fowl" (67). Chesnutt notes several instances of people mistaking him for being white and that he could certainly have passed if he had chosen to do so. He, however, did not, claiming instead to be a "voluntary Negro" ("Post-Bellum" 194). Although Harris's experience is in no way as dramatic as Chesnutt's, he played with racial crossing as well. Robert Hemenway explains that "in mimicking black speech, often calling himself Uncle Remus, signing his letters Uncle Remus, Joel Chandler Harris assumed an identity well suited to the 'other fellow' dualism of his creative life. By donning the black mask of Uncle Remus, Harris liberated a part of himself" (17). In taking on a black persona, Harris suggests the possibility of racial crossing. Although Chesnutt considered his race a "personal matter," the Uncle Julius stories likewise hint at the possibility that the line between races was thinner than Americans wanted to believe ("Post-Bellum" 194).

***

If storytelling works and the audience gets the joke and becomes part of the inner community, the final step in oral tradition is for the story to be passed on; the listener must become a teller. Joel Chandler Harris never gets to this step; the few hints that the little boy understands the stories do not result in the little boy being able or willing to repeat the stories. Instead, Harris went on to publish more collections of stories in the same formula with Uncle Remus and at times a cast of other ex-slaves telling stories to the little boy. Charles Chesnutt, however, does push his exploration of racial crossing through storytelling to this last step when John becomes the storyteller in "The Dumb Witness," a story not included in the collection, *The Conjure Woman*, because it does not involve conjure. It is the only Uncle Julius story that is not told in his voice. Eric Sundquist argues that John's telling of the story is an act of "conjure or theft" and a "silencing of Julius's voice and of Viney's story" (*To Wake* 391). He connects the method of having John tell Julius's story to the content of Viney's tongue being mutilated and finds that the story focuses on "cultural suppression" (392). Peter Schmidt critiques Sundquist's reading by questioning his assumptions about what Chesnutt's "proper material" was: "Sundquist's arguments also suggest that Chesnutt did not have a *right* to investigate John's voice" (85).

If we pay attention to Chesnutt's exploration of oral tradition, John's storytelling is not a silencing of Julius's voice but a furthering of the story. After John has visited the Murchison plantation and witnessed a confrontation between Malcolm Murchison and Viney, he asks Julius to tell him the story behind the conflict. John then tells the reader, "Some of the facts of this strange story—circumstances of which Julius was ignorant, though he had the main facts correct—I learned afterward from other sources, but I have woven them all together here in orderly sequence" ("Dumb Witness" 156). Sundquist finds that John "absorbs the tale" and tells it in his own voice but that "John's comprehension of the tale turns out to be painfully inadequate" (*To Wake* 391). To Sundquist, John takes Julius's tales and incorporates it into his own story, the same process involved in creating the "plantation mythology of post-Reconstruction" (391). But we do not have to see John's taking of the story as cultural appropriation; he takes some of the facts of the story from Julius and learns other facts from other sources. He does, in fact, what tellers normally do in oral tradition; he takes a story he has been told and shapes it according to his taste, in this case by adding information and putting the information in an "orderly sequence." He retells the story his way. As Robert Stepto argues, the implication of John telling the story is that "John had fully completed his apprenticeship as a listener" ("Simple" 51). Julius's voice, his "own quaint dialect" as John notes, is lost, but it is a necessary loss if John is going to move from being simply the audience commanding a performance to the actual performer.

He does not, in fact, turn the story into a plantation myth, as Sundquist argues, because in his telling John shows that he is part of the inside group; he is sympathetic to Viney's story. As John first arrives at the Murchison place, he describes in detail the decay evident in the entrance, which "evidently once possessed some pretensions to elegance," but now consisted of rusted fragments ("Dumb Witness" 153). The garden now "grew in wild and tangled profusion," and the house is in disrepair with the roof sinking in and several of the windows out. The place is, in short, a mess. John also provides some background information on the ancestors of the current Murchison, Malcolm. This might be part of that information John gets from sources other than Julius, and it is certainly not flattering to the white family.[11] Malcolm inherited the place from his uncle Roger who "was fond of cards, of fast horses, of rare wines, and of gay society" (156). Although Malcolm is more interested in the daily operations of the plantation, he still keeps the house as a "bachelor's hall" (157). John explains that Malcolm's main vice is "avarice" and that "perhaps it was this characteristic that kept him from marrying" (157). John thus suggests that the Murchison family was morally corrupt. When Malcolm finally decides to get married, Viney tells his intended fiancée something that causes her to break the engagement, probably the fact that Viney is Malcolm's mistress as well as his blood relative, both facts that reveal the immoral history of the family. John describes Malcolm's revenge as revealing the "worst passions of weak humanity," and when Malcolm mutilates Viney's tongue to silence her, John notes, "no angel of mercy stayed his hand" (158). Throughout his descriptions John distances himself from this white family and from the actions of Malcolm. What is more telling, however, is that he is sympathetic to Viney. After Malcolm hurts Viney, he receives word of his uncle's death and finds out that only Viney knows where the uncle's important papers are hidden. Peter Schmidt points out that when John is telling the scene of Malcolm's asking Viney where the papers are, John takes on Viney's point of view (88). John suggests that "a closer observer than Malcolm Murchison might have detected at this moment another change in the woman's expression. Perhaps it was in her eyes more than elsewhere; for into their black depths there sprang a sudden fire" ("Dumb Witness" 159). Not only, however, does John take Viney's point of view, he also embellishes the story to tell this scene. It is John who imagines that "fire" in Viney's eyes, as he suggests "perhaps" that is where her anger is manifest. John has certainly come a long way, since his first response to Uncle Julius's stories was asking whether they are true. Now he is taking on the role of storyteller shaping the tale and using his imagination instead of his reason.

At the end of the story, John and Julius make another visit to the Murchison place and find it radically changed. Order has been restored with the house repaired, a new gate hung, and the gardens cut back. Julius explains to John that Murchison died and his nephew is now renovating the place. John sees Viney on the front porch and asks to speak to the young Murchison. When she answers, "Yes, sir . . . I'll call him," John is astonished that she can in fact speak, despite her long pretense of not being able to tell where the papers were because of her mutilated mouth. Julius tells John that once Malcolm was dead, Viney told the nephew where the papers were. Julius offers John a guess at the location. When John gives up, Julius reveals that the papers were in the chair Malcolm sat in "all dese years" (163). Although John tells the story in his own voice, Julius still gets the punch line; John may sympathize with Viney, but he still does not understand the situation as well as Julius. This could mean that John is still not fully an insider and not fully a storyteller. Peter Schmidt, however, asks, "If John truly believed Viney was speechless, why did he address her in the final scene?" (90). Schmidt reads John as, at least unconsciously, aware of Viney's revenge, although John lets Julius speak for him: "John's silence may be witness to hidden feelings he cannot acknowledge in the postwar South" (90). Whether or not he is aware before this scene of Viney's ability to speak, John does seem to play along with the game at the end of discovering the secret. Julius is "grinning and chuckling to himself," but John seems to join in the humor by wanting to know the punch line. He says, "I give it up," as one would say to find the answer to a joke. That punch line is indeed the "snapper" Twain likes at the end of a humorous story, as Julius explains that the very thing Malcolm was searching for was right under him. John asks for this answer by saying, "Enlighten me" ("Dumb Witness" 163). John, as the white outside character earlier so suspicious of storytelling because of his rationality, ironically asks Julius to give him enlightenment. Julius may get to tell the punch line, but Julius and John share the humor at the end.

***

In the essay "Change the Joke and Slip the Yoke" Ralph Ellison writes a response to Stanley Edgar Hyman's essay on the connection between African American literature and folklore. Ellison is particularly disturbed by Hyman's suggestions that readers should "approach Negro folklore through the figure Hyman calls the 'darky' entertainer" (47). Ellison rejects the connection of minstrel comedy to actual African American culture. He finds that it derives, instead, from "the Anglo-Saxon branch of American folklore" (47). He sees a further danger in making the trickster figure a specifically "Negro" archetype. Ellison instead argues that the trickster strategy of being smart but playing dumb is an American one, and he connects it to the practice of masking: "Masking is a play upon possibility and ours is a society in which possibilities are many. When American life is most American it is apt to be most theatrical" (54). Ellison traces Americans masking from the colonists dressing as Indians at the Boston Tea Party to Faulkner pretending to be just a farmer. The joke in all of this, Ellison finds, is that the white man does not see himself as aligned with the black man in this masking strategy. Ellison writes, "On his side of the joke the Negro looks at the white man and finds it difficult to believe that the 'grays'—a Negro term for white people—can be so absurdly self-deluded over the true interrelatedness of blackness and whiteness" (55).

Harris's and Chesnutt's texts are filled with maskings. Joel Chandler Harris poses as Uncle Remus, who tells stories about revolution that are masked as animal tales. Charles Chesnutt uses Uncle Julius to tell stories about slavery, but the atrocities are masked by fictional elements of conjure, and his audience is masked by their suspicions of his motives. When Chesnutt and Harris are writing in the post–Civil War period, the minstrel tradition Ellison rejects and the local color school are in vogue. Both are predicated on the desire to preserve regional and racial identities, seen to be perhaps too much in flux after the war and Reconstruction. But what too often gets preserved in this time period is the figure of the "darky" that Ellison rejects. The "darky" performer was just a mask, just a clown performing to elicit a laugh. Harris and Chesnutt both start with a staple of their time period, an old "uncle" performing by telling stories, but they move past the static mask to discover the stories within. By using a frame tale and playing with oral tradition, they depict white audiences for the stories, thus making the performances dynamic and open. Chesnutt goes further than Harris in his depiction of just how much his audience can understand about the stories and the African American culture behind them, but both look to the possibilities of humor to connect audience to storyteller. They, like Twain, discover that humor in America is best told in dialect, but of the two it is probably only Chesnutt who understands the joke of the "true interrelatedness of blackness and whiteness."

2
Paradise Disrupted

William Faulkner's *Absalom, Absalom!* and Zora
Neale Hurston's *Their Eyes Were Watching God*

In the 1997 novel *Paradise*, Toni Morrison explores the desire to create a
haven in her depiction of the all-black town of Ruby, Oklahoma. Because
the eight founding families of Ruby view the world as contaminating, they
have an unwritten law against marrying outsiders, especially anyone who is
not racially pure. This insistence on containment leads to incest, as the families intermarry through the generations, and eventually to violence, as the
men of the town blame the dissolution of their community on the odd as-
sortment of women living just outside their town's borders. What Morrison clearly shows through this narrative is that the idea of paradise is dependent upon exclusion; who gets in and how is linked to who is kept out and
why.[1] In exploring paradise in an American landscape, Morrison plays with
a central myth in American literature, that of America as a kind of paradise or Eden where humans have a blank slate to start over and create a dynasty to pass down to future generations.[2] *Paradise* specifically speaks back to
William Faulkner's *Absalom, Absalom!* and Zora Neale Hurston's *Their Eyes
Were Watching God*. Jill Jones argues that *Paradise* can even be read as a "reworking" of *Absalom, Absalom!* with its focus on the project of creating a dynasty and the problems of miscegenation and incest (3). In the depiction of
an all-black town, *Paradise* also reworks the subject of Hurston's novel.[3]

Given the pervasiveness of Eden/paradise imagery in American literature, it is certainly not surprising that a major novelist like Morrison would
echo her literary predecessors. What is interesting is how she also reiterates
a more particular concern: how oral storytelling contributes to the erosion
of a paradise by questioning the master narrative. In *Paradise*, when Pat is
trying to construct a history of Ruby by writing a genealogy, a master narrative of the community, her attempts are frustrated by the dynamics of oral

tradition. All she can find to use are the snippets of gossip and stories she overhears from the other women, evidence that is not only unreliable but is also intentionally deceptive. Reading backward from *Paradise* to *Absalom, Absalom!* and *Their Eyes Were Watching God* can shed light on the role of oral storytelling in these two earlier works in disrupting the nice, neat finality of written history and thus the very walls that contain the havens and keep race lines supposedly pure.

Reading sideways from *Absalom, Absalom!* to *Their Eyes Were Watching God* also highlights the commonality in the use of oral storytelling. These two now-canonical novels were published within a year of each other (*Absalom, Absalom!* in 1936 and *Their Eyes Were Watching God* in 1937), yet outside of two articles, critics have not noticed any similarities despite the massive industry in Faulkner scholarship.[4] This lack shows the glaring need for rethinking literary categories, such as "southern literature" and "African American literature," that have tended in the past to segregate literary works.[5] Hurston and Faulkner share a historical context that actually fed their use of oral storytelling. Comparable to the 1880s and 1890s, when Joel Chandler Harris and Charles Chesnutt were writing, the decade of the 1930s was marked by a great interest in regionalism, specifically folk culture, dialect, and oral storytelling. One distinct sign of this interest is the Federal Writers' Project (FWP) of the Work Progress Administration (WPA), which mirrored and perhaps even fueled the interest in folk culture. Out of the four modern writers I will discuss in this chapter and the next, three worked for the WPA. Hurston and Ralph Ellison both worked for the FWP, collecting folklore for state guides, while Eudora Welty worked as a publicity agent taking pictures all over rural Mississippi. Only Faulkner did not have any direct involvement, although Thomas McHaney argues that Faulkner used the Mississippi guide in writing *Requiem for a Nun*, which at the very least demonstrates his awareness of the state guide series, which was the main task of the FWP. Unlike the 1880s and 1890s when regionalism was celebrated as a way of tolerating the differences in America, in the 1930s the concern was uniting citizens by educating them about their own folk heritage. This atmosphere provided the backdrop for writers such as Hurston, Faulkner, Ellison, and Welty, who then employed folk culture in their works.

Exploring folk culture in a modern era was not, however, without peril. The two white writers, Faulkner and Welty, ran the risk of appearing nostalgic or provincial by their use of oral storytelling. Contemporary reviews of Faulkner's and Welty's works attest to this risk. Leigh Anne Duck explains that some reviewers of *Absalom, Absalom!* "[described] southern culture as categorically different—in both its age and its rapid process of dissolution—

from that found elsewhere in the nation" and then "suspected that, amid such conditions, the artist or intellectual might be overwhelmed by emotional attachments to the past and trapped in a purely subjective realm, incapable of interaction with or understanding of contemporary social life" (149). With Welty's *Losing Battles* being published in 1970, thirty-four years after *Absalom, Absalom!*, the risk of Welty appearing nostalgic in exploring folk culture is even more amplified. Jonathan Yardley in his review identified nostalgia as the "motivating impulse" of the novel (36).

Hurston and Ellison as African Americans faced a different ambivalence in using oral tradition; if they employed African American storytelling, it would seem that they were playing into a white audience's desire to witness "primitive" African culture.[6] Richard Wright argues that this is indeed what Hurston does: "In the main, her novel is not addressed to the Negro, but to a white audience whose chauvinistic tastes she knows how to satisfy. She exploits the phase of Negro life which is 'quaint,' the phase which evokes a piteous smile on the lips of the 'superior' race" (17). Wright's version of the appropriate avenue of African American writing is echoed later in Houston A. Baker Jr.'s reading of *Invisible Man*, which he argues "provides only an accommodationist black folk populace" ("Failed" 5).

Not only do the writers have to worry about nostalgia or degradation, regionalism in its celebration of the particular contrasts the values of modernism. If the writers are too embedded in the local, regional, or, to use a historically loaded term, agrarian, they might be out of step with their literary counterparts. The rising prominence of modernist values ends up giving local color its resulting diminutive status. Defenders of these writers often argue that their works transcend their regional or racial identity to become universal and assumedly more valued. Philip Weinstein, for example, asks, "Is it too much to say that Faulkner is regional in his very bones, and that he reaches the universal . . . by leaping directly from the South to the world, bypassing, so to speak, the West that is in between?" ("'Make It New'" 353). Tellingly Weinstein's question is whether Faulkner jumps over the West to get to the universal; that he must leap from the South and from the space of the regional is already assumed.

The ambivalence in the historical and critical contexts about regionalism mirrors the tension between oral storytelling and the written narrative that exists in *Absalom, Absalom!* and *Their Eyes Were Watching God*. This tension then erupts into an all-out war in the later novels of Ellison and Welty. Oral storytelling drawn from folk culture fights against the written narrative in its assertions of mastery and finality. In Faulkner's and Hurston's novels the fight is played out in the desire to create a paradise with a carefully controlled narrative versus the plurality of voices telling different stories that undermine that paradise. The line between the master narrative of paradise and the excluded but powerful oral stories is literally drawn in blood. Both novels' versions of paradise depend on the problematic task of drawing race lines. Although paradise itself depends on the lines being impenetrable, the texts seem to hide from the true horror of having to examine the blood to draw the lines. In *Absalom, Absalom!* the plot turns on the possible drop of black blood in Thomas Sutpen's first son, Charles Bon. Although Bon is the pivotal character, he does not tell any part of the story and seems more specter than person. His possible racial identity is revealed only at the end of the book. In *Their Eyes Were Watching God* Janie lives in Eatonville and then in the Everglades, which the novel refers to as "the muck," surrounded only by black characters and stories, but ends up being tried by an all-white jury for murder. Race in both books indeed matters, but the texts distract from its presence until the end. In both books, it is in fact the reader who must finally declare its existence.

Toni Morrison in her reworking of the material reverses the order by announcing in the first sentence of her book, "They shoot the white girl first," thus overtly declaring race to be the key issue (*Paradise* 3). Morrison, however, never identifies which of the women living at the convent is in fact white. The reader might continue hunting for the drop of white blood or see that a paradise created on any ideal blood ends in the violence that Morrison foregrounds with this first sentence. *Paradise* in its underscoring and then erasing of race points back to the central presence and absence of race in *Absalom, Absalom!* and *Their Eyes Were Watching God*. The battle lines between white and black might be an attempt to separate paradise from the outside, but Faulkner's and Hurston's works both depict oral storytelling as a powerful force that disrupts the written text and questions a paradise created through exclusion.

***

Thomas Sutpen and Joe Starks have much in common in their ruthless drive to create dynasties that will attest to their power. One of the few critics who compare *Absalom, Absalom!* and *Their Eyes Were Watching God*, Margaret Bauer finds that the common denominator is "sterility, caused by the mistake of trying to build a New South on the same foundations as the old—ironically, a mistake being made in these two novels by the same groups of people who were victimized by the Old South: the poor white and the black" ("Sterile" 384). Sutpen and Starks try to create dynasties that mimic those of the elite white plantation planters before the Civil War and end up without the progeny to carry forth the project. Although Bauer's comparison is revealing, I will take a different path in examining what contributes to the failure of their plans.

In *Absalom! Absalom!* Thomas Sutpen begins with a very definite plan; as he explains to General Compson, "I had a design. To accomplish it I should require money, a house, a plantation, slaves, a family—incidentally of course, a wife" (212). He then goes about acquiring all the elements, from the money and slaves in Haiti to the house outside Jefferson. But this is not just a story of a man trying to live the American dream and get rich. Sutpen's design is in the grander narrative of establishing a paradise. Quentin imagines Sutpen and his slaves building the house: "Quentin seemed to watch them overrun suddenly the hundred square miles of tranquil and astonished earth and drag house and formal gardens violently out of the soundless Nothing and clap them down like cards upon a table beneath the up-palm immobile and pontific, creating the Sutpen's Hundred, the *Be Sutpen's Hundred* like the olden-time *Be Light*" (4). In Quentin's description the plantation is constructed out of a "soundless Nothing" like Eden suddenly appearing from the void.[7] Although Sutpen seems to have pulled some crafty trick by winning the house like a gambler clapping down the cards, he also plays the role of God in creating Sutpen's Hundred by seemingly speaking it into existence.

In *Their Eyes Were Watching God*, Joe Starks has a very definite plan with biblical overtones as well. The first time he meets Janie, he tells her that he is headed to Florida because he "heard all about 'em makin' a town all outa colored folks," and he wanted to "be a big voice" (28). Joe has saved $300 working for white people but sees his chance here to construct a dynasty of his own in a place where the white people will not have the power. When he and Janie arrive in the all-black town, he is dismayed to find that it is little more than a few run-down houses, but he immediately sets his plan in motion, buying land, building a store and a road, and establishing a post office. Joe's favorite phrase, "I god," indicates that he sees himself as a creator establishing a kind of paradise, starting with a blank slate and building a town over which he will preside.

For both Sutpen and Starks the symbol of their achievement is a grand house, the literal embodiment of their wealth and power. Joe Starks connects building and power in his initial vision. In this place "dat colored folks was buildin' theirselves," he could have power because "de man dat built things oughta boss it" (28). He certainly follows through when he builds his house: "It had two stories with porches, with banisters and such things," and unlike the other houses in the town, which were unpainted, the house is a "gloaty, sparkly white. The kind of promenading white that the houses of Bishop Whipple, W. B. Jackson, and the Vanderpool's wore" (47). This list of people links Starks with those wealthy enough to paint their houses, and his idea works. The house itself gives him power; the "bow-down command in his face" is made "more tangible" because of his intimating house.

Thomas Sutpen also begins his project with a house. It takes him two years with his "crew of imported slaves" working "from sunup to sundown" to complete the house, a "dream of grim and castlelike magnificence" (*Absalom*, 28–29). He later brings the materials needed to furnish the house, from crystal chandeliers to mahogany furniture, so vast and costly that one member of the town, Akers, claims "he stole the whole durn steamboat," and Sutpen is arrested based upon these suspicions (34).

To create such a magnificent house, Sutpen hires—or enslaves (as many of the narrators seem to suggest)—a French architect, who, as Alex Vernon points out, "remains the novel's most critically neglected character" (158). His presence in the novel is indeed puzzling. Vernon suggests that he plays the foil to the Haitian slaves: "The unnamed French architect represents [Sutpen's] overly civilized soul, the Dr. Jekyll to the slaves' collective Hyde" (158).[8] But one particular episode in which the architect tries to escape and Sutpen hunts him down suggests that the architect plays yet another role. The chase is described as a hunt for a runaway slave, with Sutpen using dogs to scent the trail and enlisting the help of the other men in Jefferson to help him retrieve the architect. No one suggests that the architect is white and not bound, which would, therefore, free him to flee; even when he is caught, he seems resigned to his fate and goes back to finish the house. Sean Latham argues that even though the image evokes the hunt for a black slave, the "architect is never fully identified in the text with a black slave" because he "utilizes his unique knowledge of physics to effect a number of creative gambits for eluding his pursuers" (457). The architect, however, comes very close to being colored black in this episode. His dress changes from the overly civilized, "his embroidered vest and Fauntleroy tie and a hat like a Baptist congressman," to dirty rags, "with one sleeve missing from his frock coat and his flowered vest ruined by water and mud where he had fallen in the river and one pants leg ripped down so they could see where he had tied up his leg with a piece of his shirt tail and the rag bloody and the leg swollen, and his hat was completely gone" (*Absalom*, 206). Although his face shows his "will to endure," when they hand him a bottle of water, he takes it "in one of his little dirty coon-like hands" (207). The architect has not only lost the markers of civilization such as a hat, he is described as "coon-like," a racial slur for blacks. That the architect of the very house that is supposed to stand as a symbol of paradise becomes black hints that something is amiss with the construction project.

Both Sutpen and Starks in fact set up their projects based on the containment of racial crossing; they dream of paradises based on exclusion but, as the French architect hints, white too easily becomes black and black becomes white. Sutpen's idea is sparked by an act of exclusion. He tells General Compson the story of how his family slowly drifted down over time from their mountain home and somehow landed at a plantation. As a boy Sutpen is fascinated by the white owner who "lived in the biggest house he had even seen and spent most of the afternoon . . . in a barrel stave hammock between two trees, with his shoes off" (184). So Sutpen is delighted the day his father tells him to take a message to the big house because he thinks he will get to see inside it. The abrupt dismissal by the "monkey nigger" shocks him; instead of showing him inside, the butler tells him to go around to the back door, which is the first time it occurs to Sutpen that he is not good enough to see inside the white owner's house. This exclusion sparks Sutpen's plan; he could not shoot the white owner, so he decides instead to become him: "You got to have land and niggers and a fine house to combat them with" (192).[9] After abandoning his first wife once he has money from his marriage to her, he turns away his own son, Charles Bon, because Charles did not fit Sutpen's design, probably because of his race. Sutpen's paradise is the plantation house with the white family inside and the black slaves working outside; letting Charles Bon into the family would destroy the containment he sought.

Joe Starks does not have to worry about whites invading the haven of the all-black town, but he still focuses on exclusion as a way of asserting and demonstrating his power. He excludes Janie from the rest of the community as a way of showing the class distinction between himself and the rest of Eatonville. When Joe opens his new store in the center of the town, he tells Janie to dress up because "she must look on herself as the bell-cow, the other women were the gang" (*Their Eyes* 41). While Janie would love to spend her time on the porch listening to the storytelling, Joe insists she stay in the store, away from the "trashy people" (54).[10] Janie reflects Joe's status, so keeping her apart from the community shows his power over them. Joe Starks's exclusion rests on class, but, as I will argue, the problem of race lies right under the surface.

In fact the irony in both men's designs is that they become the very things they tried to exclude. In Eatonville Starks may feel that he needs to show his power through class since everyone is the same race, but his neighbors wonder if he has indeed become a little too "white." That "gloaty, sparkly

white" house he builds looks too much like the "big house" on the plantation and "the rest of the town looked like the servants' quarters" surrounding it (47). The town becomes disconcerted as well by the fancy spit cups
he and Janie use and concludes, "It was bad enough for white people, but
when one of your own color could be so different it put you on a wonder.
It was like seeing your sister turn into a 'gator. A familiar strangeness. You
keep seeing your sister in the 'gator and the 'gator in your sister, and you'd
rather not" (48). The imagery is of a human becoming an animal, but the
suggestion is that Starks is becoming white. When Hicks feels threatened by
Starks's power because Starks claims he will set up a post office, Hicks emphasizes his race, calling him a "stray darky" and a "colored man" (39), and
when Starks wants the town to build a drainage ditch, the men "murmured
hotly about slavery being over" (47). Joe Starks may appear to be one of
them except for his wealth, but the distinction takes on the overtones of a racial difference. When Thomas Sutpen is working furiously day and night to
build the very house that is a symbol of his design, he and his slaves remain
covered in mud as a protection from the mosquitoes and are "distinguishable
one from another by his beard and eyes alone" (*Absalom*, 28). The difference
becomes negligible. Both when he qualms the slave revolt in Haiti and when
he fights with his "wild niggers" for sport, he seems to have some uncanny
connection with them. At least for Rosa, he becomes a "beast"; the animal
imagery, as in *Their Eyes Were Watching God*, seems to signal racial crossing.
He becomes yet a different creature for Quentin, as Quentin muses that Sutpen "would have accepted the necessary discomfort and even pain of the bri-
ers and thorns in a thicket if the thicket could have given him the protection
he sought" (11). Sutpen playing Brer Rabbit might just be a black person dis-
guised as white. It is hard to create a paradise when in your attempt to get rid
of the Other, you have to become that Other, as both Sutpen and Starks do.

The dynasties eventually fall apart to the great dismay of both protagonists. In Sutpen's case his son Henry commits murder and flees from his
father's grand house leaving no one to inherit the dynasty, although little
is left after the ravages of the Civil War. If Quentin and Shreve are correct
and Charles Bon is Thomas Sutpen's first son, then Henry actually commits
fratricide, and the Eden Sutpen creates has the biblical echo of brother killing brother. The Civil War is an appropriate backdrop for this fall since the
model Sutpen used for his paradise was the plantation worked by slave labor. The house itself also reflects the loss. Quentin and Shreve imagine that
when Sutpen turned Bon away that "he must have felt and heard the design—
house, position, posterity and all—come down like it had been built out of
smoke, making no sound, creating no rush of displaced air and not even leav-

ing any debris" (215). From that point forward the house, in an echo of the Gothic houses of Hawthorne and Poe, falls into ruin, until Quentin comments on its current "smell of desolation and decay" (293).[11] The grand finale then seems more like denouement when Clytie burns the house down, fearing that the ambulance Rosa sent to help the ailing Henry is the police coming to arrest him for murder. In Joe Starks's case, Janie finally refuses to be the symbol of his power in part because her definition of power is different from his. When Joe overhears her bemoaning the treatment of Matt Bonner's mule and buys it to let it rest, Janie tells him, "Freein' dat mule makes uh mighty big man outa you. Something like George Washington and Lincoln. Abraham Lincoln, he had the whole United States tuh rule so he freed de Negroes. You got uh town so you freed uh mule. You have tuh have power tuh free things and dat makes you lak uh king uh something" (*Their Eyes* 58). To Janie, power should work toward freedom not containment. After years of putting up with Joe's restrictions, Janie lashes out by insulting him publicly in the store: "When you pull down yo' britches, you look lak de change uh life" (79). By comparing him to an old woman, Janie emasculates him, and Joe realizes that even "good-for-nothing's" would not consider him powerful anymore. After her public insult, Joe becomes ill and dies leaving no children to inherit his hard-earned dynasty.

In their design, rise, and fall, Sutpen and Starks have followed the same path. They also make the same critical mistake: they think that their vision of paradise is so large and grand that they can control other people to attain it. For Sutpen, although he and some of the later narrators chalk his failure up to his "innocence," the problem centers more on that "incidentally" he uses to describe his need for a wife; his family members are not content to remain "incidental" like props on a set.[12] Charles Bon wants to be acknowledged, Judith wants to marry Charles, Henry initially chooses his friend over his family but then murders him. Judith's metaphor of the loom fits Sutpen's problem well: "You are born at the same time with a lot of other people, all mixed up with them, like trying to, having to, move your arms and legs with strings only the same strings are hitched to all the other arms and legs and the others all trying and they dont know why either except that the strings are all in one another's way like five or six people all trying to make a rug on the same loom only each one wants to weave his own pattern into the rug" (100–101). In Starks's case he cannot control the one person, his wife, Janie, he needs to control in order to show the town his ultimate power. He can keep her off the porch and make her hide her hair, but he cannot ultimately control her thoughts. For both Starks and Sutpen, the exclusions they make to build their paradises come back to haunt them in the end. Joe Starks tries to set up exclusions based on class, but when he gets ill, Janie notices that "people who never had known what it was to enter the gate of the Mayor's yard unless it were to do some menial job now paraded in and out as his confidants" (83). The very house that suggested that he was playing the role of the white master is now open to everyone in the town. Sutpen went to great lengths to establish a racially pure family (if we take Quentin's and Shreve's version as truth) by leaving his first wife, denying his first son, and then turning that son away again. But for all his effort, his one living descendant at the end of the book is Jim Bond, the grandchild of Charles Bon and his octoroon mistress. In Morrison's novel the men of the town resort to violence in their attempt to maintain control; they supposedly shoot all the women at the convent, but like Starks and Sutpen, their control and the paradise they build upon it vanishes as the bodies of the women seemingly vanish after the riot. The walls of each paradise come tumbling down.

***

The lack of control comes not just from other people asserting their own designs but from the many different individuals who narrate the story of paradise in both novels. Henry Louis Gates Jr. has coined the term "speakerly" to describe Hurston's novel, but the ability of a written text to mimic oral storytelling is illustrated in *Absalom, Absalom!* as well. The oral traditions that Faulkner and Hurston draw from are different, and I do not want to flatten the distinctions between southern white and African American cultures, but, as I argued in my analysis of Chesnutt and Harris, the traditions are not entirely separate. Both Hurston and Faulkner, for example, play with the form of the frame tale that they inherit from Harris and Chesnutt. Faulkner has the oral storytelling of Quentin and Shreve framed by a written narrative, the letter that Mr. Compson sends to Quentin at Harvard. In Hurston's use of the frame tale, she revises the place of the narrator by writing the frame as the oral storytelling in Janie's voice and the middle section as the terrain of the third-person narrator. The methods that Faulkner and Hurston use to include multiple voices differ, with Faulkner's layers of narrators and Hurston's experiment with free indirect discourse, but the effect, I will argue, is the same; multiple tellers equal decentralized power, so oral storytelling undermines the construction of paradise.

Over and over again in Faulkner criticism is the assertion that *Absalom, Absalom!* has four narrators, Rosa, Mr. Compson, Quentin, and Shreve, with analyses of their biases, their different structures, their relative reliability, and so on.[13] But not enough attention has been paid to the layers of narrators underneath these four; their stories of Thomas Sutpen rest on the oral story-telling of scores of other people in the town of Jefferson. In the first section that Rosa narrates to Quentin, she describes herself overhearing conversations about the events she relates instead of witnessing them herself. She develops her opinion of Thomas Sutpen as an ogre "out of the overheard talk of adults," most likely her father and aunt. She hears about the Sutpens' wild carriage ride to church from listening at the door to her aunt and father debating whether he should interfere in Ellen's marriage. She learns more about that marriage by overhearing her father's feeble attempt at interference and Ellen's refusal to discuss her husband. Finally after narrating the story of Judith hiding in the loft to watch her father fight with the slaves, Rosa admits, "But I was not there. I was not there to see the two Sutpen faces this time—once on Judith and once on the negro girl beside her—looking down through the square entrance to the loft" (22). Rosa is not telling the story to Quentin as much as she is retelling the story. In chapter 5, even though Rosa is now recounting events she actually witnessed and does not have to rely on what she has simply overheard, she still alludes to other tellers. In fact, her whole story is set up in reaction to the stories of nameless others, whom she is sure have told Quentin everything: "So they will have told you doubtless already how I told that Jones to take that mule which was not his around to the barn and harness it to our buggy while I put on my hat and shawl and locked the house" (107). She is again retelling a story because it has "already" been told, although she then proceeds to tell what "they" cannot know. Her version is set up in contrast to the one she is sure "they" have already told Quentin: "Oh yes, I know 'Rosie Coldfield, lose him, weep him; caught a man but couldn't keep him'" (136).

Mr. Compson gives a bit more information on who this "they" might be. Although some of his narrative comes directly from his father, General Compson, he also refers continually to "the town" as his source for the story. It was "the town" that learned Sutpen bought a hundred acres, and it was "the town" that learned the French architect came from Martinique. Who exactly makes up the "the town" is never specified; for example, when Mr. Compson is telling the story of Sutpen driving through town with a wagon full of slaves, he only says that "someone (not General Compson) [looked] beneath the wagon hood and into a black tunnel filled with still eyeballs and smelling like a wolfden" (27). Nor is there an indication of how many story-tellers make up the oral tradition of "the town"; perhaps it is the entire population of the town and its surroundings, which Faulkner's map at the end gives as "Whites 6298 Negroes 9313." The second part of this rubric may, in fact, be the crucial one. It is only through the "cabin-to-cabin whispering of negroes" that the town learns of the explosion on Christmas Eve that led to Henry and Charles riding away together (84). Later Mr. Compson claims that General Compson learns of Charles Etienne Saint-Valery Bon's return with a black wife "by that country grapevine whose source is among the negroes" (166). How much of the vague "town's" knowledge is indeed rooted in this oral storytelling we can only speculate, but at the very least a number of unnamed narrators participate in an oral storytelling that provides the basis for Rosa and Mr. Compson's stories, and, at the very most, if the entire population, white and black, is counted, perhaps even up to fifteen thousand. Quentin and Shreve then add two more layers on to the pile. By chapter 6, Shreve tells Quentin a story that Quentin has already told Shreve, that Mr. Compson told Quentin, that "grandfather" or General Compson told Mr. Compson, that the town and that "country grapevine" has told grandfather. So many different tellers have a chance to shape this story, there is no ability to control or contain it. The many narrators have a devastating effect on Quentin in particular, who, in trying to construct the story of Sutpen, seems doomed: "His very body was an empty hall echoing with sonorous defeated names; he was not a being, an entity, he was a commonwealth. He was a barracks filled with stubborn back-looking ghosts" (7). In this book the living and the dead get in on the telling.

In *Their Eyes Were Watching God* the multiple narrators occur because of a split in the narrative between the first-person narrator, Janie, and the third-person narrator who helps tell Janie's story as well as the stories of other characters. This split has been the subject of much critical debate. Robert Stepto was the first critic to complain about Hurston's experiment. He argues that the split is a "flaw" because "Hurston's curious insistence on having Janie's tale—her personal history in and as literary form—told by an omniscient third person, rather than by a first-person narrator, implies that Janie has not really won her voice and self after all—that her author (who is, quite likely, the omniscient narrative voice) cannot see her way clear to giving Janie her voice outright" (*From Behind* 166). Lillie P. Howard points out that it seems awkward because "in some places . . . much of what Janie tells Pheoby, Pheoby must already know, partly because she is Janie's best friend, and partly because Pheoby was a part of Eatonville just as Janie was. Both must have had many common experiences which there would be no need to repeat in the narrative" (94). Others critics disagree, claiming that the novel is multivocal and in the call-and-response tradition. Cathy Brigham argues that "political empowerment" through first-person voice is not the focus anyway (402).[14] The most developed answer is in Henry Louis Gates Jr.'s *The Signifying Monkey*, in which he comes up with the term "speakerly" and examines how the text "[emulates] the phonetic, grammatical, and lexical structures of actual speech, an emulation designed to produce the illusion of oral narration" (196). *Their Eyes Were Watching God* has straight dialogue such as in the porch scenes between Janie and Pheoby, speeches given in dialect such as Tony Taylor's speech at the opening of Joe's store, free indirect discourse when the narrator shares the point of view of Janie or Joe or even one of the minor characters such as Sop-de-Bottom, and storytelling such as the stories about Matt Bonner's mule. The effect of the structure is that the text's subject is larger than Janie's story of herself; it is then by extension much larger than the story of Joe. The multiple narrators mean that Joe's rise to wealth and power does not make him the sole, or even the most important, protagonist. He cannot in the end control the story.

Although Faulkner and Hurston choose different methods to replicate the multiple narrators inherent in oral storytelling, the effect on Thomas Sutpen and Joe Starks is the same: a loss of power. Not only can Sutpen and Starks not contain the story of their pursuit of paradise, they both show themselves to be poor storytellers. Joe does a fairly good job telling a story about God as the "Sun-Maker" when he unveils the first street light in Eatonville. The crowd responds by singing a hymn and everyone seem inspired, but later Joe is unable to use his voice to gain power. After Janie asserts her version of power in comparing Joe to Lincoln and Hambo responds by proclaiming her a "born orator," Joe only bites his cigar and "never said a word" (58). After Janie's public insult, Joe hits her because he "didn't know the words for all this, but he knew the feeling" (80). Joe succeeds in becoming wealthy but does not gain that "big voice" he desired. Thomas Sutpen tells part of his story to General Compson (and the reader hears it as Quentin retells it to Shreve as Mr. Compson retold it to Quentin), but he leaves out crucial information. When Sutpen forms his plan to become like the white plantation owner, he goes to the West Indies to acquire the money. Quentin comments that "that's how he said it: not how he managed to find where the West Indies were nor where ships departed from to go there, nor how he got to where the ships were and got in one nor how he liked the sea nor about the hardships of a sailor's life" (193). Then he does not say what exactly it was about his first wife he discovered that caused him to leave her. Quentin again comments, "He was telling some more of it, already into what he was telling yet still without telling how he got to where he was nor even how what he was now involved in . . . came to occur" (198). After describing the riot (but not how he subdued the slaves), Sutpen abruptly stops. Thirty years later he tells a bit more to General Compson but never offers a coherent narrative.[15] Both Sutpen and Joe are simply unable to use their voice to construct a narrative; the many other voices crowding in to tell other versions or even other stories then make the containment of paradise to one design impossible.

***

The inclusion of oral storytelling in the two novels additionally shifts attention away from the subject of building a paradise to the performance of the story; the focus is not the *what* but the *how*. While this is certainly true for Thomas Sutpen, as the various narrators perform the story and the listeners pay attention to the performance itself, it is even more so for Joe Starks, who plays only one part of the story of Janie's life, but then the novel shifts focus even away from Janie's life to the performance of the story of her life. That it is not the content of the story that is important is signaled in both novels by the undercutting of the suspense of the plot. In *Their Eyes Were Watching God*, the ending of the story actually appears on the first page, Janie comes back into town "from burying the dead" (1). Although Hurston does not reveal until much later that it is Tea Cake who died, the ending to Janie's story is evident from the beginning. In *Absalom, Absalom!* the sense of plot is undercut by the lack of newness in its telling. Sparked by Quentin receiving Mr. Compson's letter, Quentin and Shreve begin discussing the saga of Sutpen, but Shreve has already heard the story; they then rehearse the story, adding on additional elements to enhance its dramatic appeal. Quentin has heard the story so many times he even complains, "*I am going to have to hear it all over again I am already hearing it all over again I am listening to it all over again*" (222). This focus on the performance of the narrative will then even further diminish the power to contain the subject that is the tangible paradise, resulting, in both novels, in the tension between the written narrative and the oral storytelling.

In *Their Eyes Were Watching God* Joe is dead by the middle of the novel and the reader follows Janie as she enjoys her widowhood and then marries Tea Cake. Joe's story certainly gets subsumed in the larger novel, but then, at many points, so does Janie's, as the text contains episodes of storytelling just for the fun of it. As the narrator explains, the storytelling "never ended because there was no end to reach. It was a contest in hyperbole and carried on for no other reason" (63). The emphasis on the performance of the story is exemplified in Dave and Jim's storytelling about their love for Daisy.[16] Dave starts the rhetorical contest off by challenging Jim: "We'll prove right now who love dis gal de best. How much time is you willin' tuh make fuh Daisy?" (68). When Jim answers, "Twenty yeahs!" Dave responds, "Me, Ah'll beg de Judge tuh hang me, and wouldn't take nothin' less than life" (69). When

Jim tells Daisy that he would buy her a steamship, Dave tells her, "Uh lil ole steamship! Daisy, Ah'll take uh job of cleanin' out de Atlantic Ocean fuh you any time you say you so desire" (69). Jim counters by telling her, "If Ah wuz ridin' up in uh earoplane way up in de sky and Ah looked down and seen you walkin' and knowed you'd have tuh walk ten miles tuh get home, Ah'd step backward offa dat earoplane just to walk home wid you" (69). Everyone on the porch knows that Jim and Dave are not really offering to do any great feats; the stories are just "acting-out courtship and everybody is in the play" (67). The audience is listening not to how much Jim and Dave love Daisy, but to how well they can construct stories of love. These stories do not help further the plot, if the plot is supposed to be Janie's story, nor do the mule stories that take such a prominent place in the text.

The town loves to tell stories about Matt Bonner's malnourished mule to poke fun at Bonner's stinginess. Sam tells the story of women using the mule's sides as a washboard: "Yeah, Matt, dat mule so skinny tell de women is usin' his rib bones fuh uh rub-board and hangin' things out on his hockbones tuh dry" (52). Not to be outdone, Lige tells the story of the mule chasing a child in the street until "all of de sudden de wind changed and blowed de mule way off his course, him bein' so poor and everything, and before de ornery varmint could take, de youngun had done got over de fence" (53). Although Matt claims that he does feed his mule adequately and protests the stories, the town continues telling the stories: "Everybody indulged in the mule talk. He was next to the Mayor in prominence, and made better talking" (53). The story of Joe gets ignored in favor of the performance of the mule stories. The series of mule stories climax at the "draggin'-out" of the mule's body, which the townpeople turn into a grand performance of a mock funeral. Joe and Sam remark on "our most distinguished citizen" with the other men and women acting out their part as mourners (60). The scene shows storytelling as sheer performance as the people "made great ceremony over the mule" and "mocked everything human in death" (60). In "Characteristics of Negro Expression," Zora Neale Hurston explains the penchant of African Americans to turn stories and events into drama: "Every phase of Negro life is highly dramatized. No matter how joyful or sad the case there is sufficient poise for drama. Everything is acted out" (39). In her portrayal of the mock-funeral performance, Hurston depicts the performance of language becoming the primary focus. In Sam's stories he imitates both a schoolteacher and the local preacher while "the sisters got mock-happy and shouted and had to be held up by the menfolks" (*Their Eyes* 61).

The funeral scene then leads into the one truly bizarre episode in *Their Eyes Were Watching God*, the buzzard funeral. The buzzards get the last laugh by imitating the people in their imitation of a funeral complete with a buzzard "Parson," who stands on the mule. The chorus's answer of "Bare, bare fat" to the repeated question, "What killed this man?" alludes to the people's stories of the mule's malnourishment and their humorous constructions of his character. If the townspeople "mocked everything human in death" in their mock funeral, the buzzards mock death itself in their consumption of the mule. The mule is not "our most distinguished citizen"; he is nothing more than a meal. The problem with the buzzard performance is that the talking buzzards are presented as a story not by a character but by the third-person narrator.[17] Hurston can do this because the text is not focused on the "truth" of what happened but on the performance of how to tell it; in a novel that invests so heavily in oral storytelling, a story about talking buzzards makes sense. But critics still struggle with the problem of tying these stories to the "subject" of Janie. Some see the mule stories as reflecting Janie's inferior status in her marriage with Joe; Nanny sets up this reading by claiming, "De nigger woman is de mule uh de world so fur as Ah can see" (14).[18] John Lowe attempts to incorporate the talking buzzard story back into the plot of Janie's life by making Janie its author: "Since Janie is telling the tale to Pheoby, this becomes *her* added touch, *her* 'mule story,' voiced at last, and also revenge against Jody, who forbade her to attend the ceremony, much less speak of it" (173). As valid as these connections may be, they expose the tension between the written narratives of Joe's vision and Janie's life story and the oral storytelling that disrupts the plot by focusing on performance alone.

Absalom, Absalom! shares the focus on how the stories are told. The four narrators (retelling the stories of the countless other narrators) are not as concerned with some grand truth of the story as much as how well they construct their particular version. Rosa shows her awareness that she is constructing her version by the references to the "they" who have already told Quentin the content of the story. In the performance she imagines "they" gave, Rosa is only a "warped biter orphaned country stick" and "the daughter merely of a small store-keeper" (136, 137). She imagines what "they" say of her broken engagement, "*And that's what she cant forgive him for: not for the insult, nor even for having jilted her: but for being dead*" (137). Rosa, in her storytelling performance, tries to craft a different version: "*But I forgave him. They will tell you different, but I did*" (138). Mr. Compson also demonstrates his awareness that he is constructing a narrative in telling three different versions of the first meeting between Henry and Charles. His story has to fit his idea that Charles had seduced Henry and thought of Judith as only "the woman vessel with which to consummate the love whose actual object was the youth" (86). The first meeting between Henry and Charles, then, has to take on a magical quality as in a Hollywood movie or a romance novel. So Mr. Compson plays with different ideas: "Henry first saw [Charles] riding perhaps through the grove at the University on one of the two horses which he kept there or perhaps crossing the campus on foot in the slightly Frenchified cloak and hat which he wore, or perhaps (I like to think this) presented formally to the man reclining in a flowered, almost feminized gown, in a sunny window in his chambers" (76). Compson's use of the word "perhaps" and his admission, "I like to think this," demonstrate his awareness that he is constructing a story and his intention, as a storyteller, to perform the story in the best possible manner.

The final two principal narrators, Quentin and Shreve, are aware of their story as a performance as they—mostly Shreve with Quentin critiquing—try to fashion events into a story about love. At the beginning their story is about the romantic love between Charles Bon and Judith, but the story keeps diverting into Charles's attempts to get Sutpen to acknowledge him and his need for fatherly love. Shreve tells the story of Charles's first trip home with Henry, when Sutpen does not even hint that he knows Charles is his son. Charles then thinks of Judith, "*She would be easy*" (258). Quentin protests, "But it's not love" (258). Shreve then decides that Charles really wanted Judith but that the possibility of incest may be underlying his desire. Quentin is still not sure and just says, "I dont know" (259). Shreve reconstructs the narrative so that Charles does not love Judith but thinks she is his fate. Henry now is the one who loves Charles and gives his life and Judith's to him. Quentin, still not satisfied, claims, "That's still not love" (263). As Quentin and Shreve try on different versions of love, they are not as concerned with the true relationship between these people as with which performance is most appealing. Shreve also invents out of thin air a lawyer in New Orleans who plots for Charles and Henry to meet. Shreve imagines that he "had the secret drawer in the secret safe and the secret paper in it" to record the events in Sutpen's life (241). The narrator suggests that the lawyer "perhaps had never existed at all anywhere" but was "probably true enough" (268). The lawyer simply makes the story better. Quentin and Shreve, along with Rosa and Mr. Compson, betray their awareness that the stories they tell are constructions and that the significance is in how well they tell their particular version.

The radical uncertainty in the plot that results from the various narrators forming their versions into performances, in addition to the layers of narrators they rely on, has led critics to wonder about the status of "truth" in the novel. Joseph W. Reed argues that the book asks the question, "What is fiction?" (146) while Colleen Donnelly argues the uncertainty points to questions about the making of history. Gerhard Hoffmann suggests that since the novel "makes history into a playing field for the imagination" then "the relationship between truth and imagination is not finally settled" (282). If we pay attention to the reliance on oral storytelling, it is both history and fiction that are questioned, as they both rely on the attention to plot. The move in *Absalom, Absalom!* is not just from history (or "truth") to fiction (or "imagination") but from the concerns of written fiction and history, what happened and who did it, to the concerns of oral storytelling, how well can the teller construct an appealing story about that what and that who.

We cannot, however, escape the fact that *Absalom, Absalom!* is a written work of fiction, as much as Faulkner plays with techniques and devices to make it seem like a live storytelling event.[19] Despite the characters' attention to construction, the murder plot (why did Henry kill Charles?) still drives the plot, and writing still frames the oral storytelling. The storytelling of Quentin and Shreve in that Harvard dorm room is framed by the letter Mr. Compson writes Quentin telling him of Rosa's death. The first part of the letter is introduced in the Harvard setting, the storytelling interrupts the letter, and then the last part of the letter occurs at the end of the book. We also have the letter Charles writes Judith during the war that Judith gives to Quentin's grandmother. Her reason for doing so points to the drive of the written narratives to record the plot. She describes a gravestone, a "block of stone with scratches on it," that "after a while they don't even remember the name and what the scratches were trying to tell and it doesn't matter" (101). Since the writing on gravestones eventually fades, Judith thinks it would be better to have the scratches on "a scrap of paper" you could give someone, as she gives the letter to Mrs. Compson, then "at least it would be something just because it would have happened. . . . it would be at least a scratch, something, something that might make a mark on something that *was* once for the reason that it can die someday" (101). Judith's vision of writing either on a gravestone or on a scrap of paper indicates the desire to record history, to assert what happened. The headstone is literalized later when Quentin visits Judith's grave with his father and reads the epitaph, "*Pause, Mortal; Remember Vanity and Folly and Beware*" (171). Even the chronology, genealogy, and map that William Faulkner adds to the end of the narrative point to the thrust of the written word toward recording history. Despite this thrust, the oral storytelling in its play with the "history" to heighten the performance disrupts the written narrative's control of the story and produces the resulting tension.

The tension spills over into the criticism as readers become historians, following the clues and pinning down the facts. Karen McPherson wonders why so many critics have been tempted to offer up yet another reading: "I would suggest that, as critics, we do not write about *Absalom, Absalom!* merely because, like Miss Rosa, 'we want it told.' We are more deeply implicated than that: we want *in on the telling*. Thus, we persist in scratching out our own inconclusive versions, refusing to let the story end" (432). While being "in on the telling" is part of the job of the listener in oral storytelling, as I will argue in the next section, trying to craft a reading that will put finality on the story runs counter to the oral nature of the tale. For both *Absalom, Absalom!* and *Their Eyes Were Watching God* we need to stand in the middle ground that Harris and Chesnutt introduce between written and oral narrative. We cannot read either novel as just a written fiction and demand coherence of plot in Hurston's novel and finality of answers in Faulkner's novel, but we also cannot treat the novels as live events because the oral storytelling is encoded in written language. Here, in fact, is where the strongest connection between the two novels lies; Faulkner and Hurston share that middle ground.

***

Oral storytelling works against written narrative's drive for plot by decentralizing power, but the power becomes even more diffused by the audiences for the stories. Oral storytelling includes the listener in the making of meaning. This inclusion, of course, runs directly counter to the exclusion required by Sutpen's and Starks's ideas of paradise. The inclusion extends from the listeners portrayed in the novels to the readers of the novels, who also play a role in determining meaning. Instead of the containment of a master narrative, both novels have the ongoing trajectory of oral tradition.

Faulkner and Hurston both use the technique, inherited from earlier writers such as Harris and Chesnutt, of having characters serve as audiences in the text not only to set up the context of oral storytelling but also to prefigure the reader's own role. The reader figuratively sits beside Quentin as he listens to Rosa and his father tell their stories and then in that Harvard room between Quentin and Shreve listening in turn to their versions. Hurston likewise puts the reader right on the store porch as the characters listen to each other's tall tales and on the back porch next to Pheoby as she serves as the example of a sympathetic listener. But readers are not just sitting; the point is that the listeners and by extension the readers are not passive. Michael Awkward explains call-and-response in African American oral tradition: "The audience not only aids a speaker's performance, but also performs in its own right. Every member of the black audience is required to participate actively in communication. The audience, in fact, is a speaker, and the speaker, thriving on the response of the audience, is a listener" (97). Although Awkward contrasts this interaction with the quiet courtesy of a Western audience, the white listener in southern oral storytelling must also speak up.

One marker of the inclusion of the reader is the teller speaking directly to the audience. In *Absalom, Absalom!* this inclusion is in part signaled by the occasional use of the second-person "you" as the teller acknowledges the audience. Rosa, for example, speaks directly to her audience to guess what Quentin might be thinking, "*I was not spying, though you will say I was,*" and at times as a way of keeping her audience from drifting away, "*Because I asked nothing of him, you see. And more than that: I gave him nothing, which is the sum of loving*" (118). If the reader is figuratively sitting next to Quentin, that "you" can mean the reader as well. Rosa does not ever let Quentin interrupt to ask questions or add information, but the possibility is there for him and the reader to disagree and form another version of the events she describes.[20] Quentin also uses the second person when he describes himself listening to his father: "*But you were not listening, because you knew it all already, had learned, absorbed it already without the medium of speech somehow from having been born and living beside it, with it, as children will and do: so that what your father was saying did not tell you anything so much as it struck, word by word, the resonant strings of remembering, who had been here before, seen these graves more than once in the rambling expeditions of boyhood whose aim was more than the mere hunting of game*" (172). Quentin is clearly speaking of himself seeing the Sutpens' graveyard, and he uses second person as a substitute for first person. However, since readers have not had the experience of seeing the graveyard, Quentin's use of "you" puts the reader in place as a listener of his father's story.

In *Their Eyes Were Watching God* the split in narrative voice helps include the reader; as Janie tells her story to Pheoby, the third-person narrator tells the story to the reader. Lillie Howard finds awkwardness in the scenes involving Pheoby if the story is Janie's narration to Pheoby. However, this awkwardness is answered if the third-person narrator's audience is the reader, who would not already know about these incidents. The narrator, for example, tells of Joe refusing to eat any food cooked by Janie, and Pheoby tells Janie that he is afraid she is trying to poison him. Pheoby and Sam discuss when Janie first starts seeing Tea Cake, and the reader is aware of Pheoby's subsequent warning to Janie. Hearing about these incidents helps the reader gain more comprehension about Janie's life. Christine Levecq argues that the narrator even "establishes complicity with readers" when the narrator comments that Janie "didn't read books so she didn't know that she was the world and the heavens boiled down to a drop" (96). The narrator "winks at the reader," who is reading a book, and thus acknowledges the reader as the audience.

Some critics, however, argue that Hurston's intended audience is limited to black readers. Thomas Cassidy, for example, contends that the novel assumes that the reader is black, "When the narrator tells us that Pearl Stone, who has been watching Janie, laughed and fell all over Mrs. Sumpkins, she does not bother to identify who Pearl Stone and Mrs. Sumpkins are, nor what color they may be. It is as if the narrator is assuming that we are a part of the community and so do not need them identified, and certainly do not need anyone to point out that they are black like everyone else" (265–66). It is not important, however, or necessary to identify these two characters any more than in their position as "porch-sitters" who criticize Janie, and if the reader has not already picked up clues that the community is an all-black town from the images and diction used, he or she soon will. Carla Kaplan takes Cassidy's assumptions even further by claiming that the reader of the novel is not only black but also a woman, idealized by Pheoby. She then reads Hurston's construction of her reader as "essentialistic" and argues that this suggests that Hurston "either could not imagine communicability across differences or that she could not imagine (or locate) the nurturant, sympathetic community in which such communication might be possible" (133–34). These critics seem to be missing the split in perspective and the middle ground. Janie does indeed find her ideal audience in her "kissin' friend" Pheoby, but the narrator is speaking to a broader audience than Pheoby, the reader of the novel, whoever he or she might be.

In both novels the inclusion occurs from more than just the clues that the reader is being addressed by the teller, although these do help set up the context. The reader of *Absalom, Absalom!* and *Their Eyes Were Watching God* must enter the story and help form the narrative. Many critics of Faulkner's novel have commented on the reader's role of sifting through the versions and providing if not complete coherence, since finality is unachievable, at least some judgment about the narrative.[21] As an audience to Quentin, Shreve provides a kind of stand-in for the reader because Shreve is an outsider, listens to Quentin's version of the story, and then retells it trying to fill in the narrative gaps.[22] If we are to be like Shreve, we would be a more active listener than Quentin is when he hears Rosa's and his father's stories. Shreve is willing to interrupt the story, as when Quentin says that Sutpen was born in West Virginia and Shreve corrects him, "Because if he was twenty-five years old in Mississippi in 1833, he was born in 1808. And there wasn't any West Virginia in 1808 because—" (179). Later Shreve even tries to take over the storytelling, but finally Shreve and Quentin tell the story together and the audience moves into the storyteller's seat.

This move is most dramatic when Quentin and Shreve are figuring out the final confrontation scene between Henry and Charles. Fiction and reality collide as the characters actually enter the story: "So that now it was not two but four of them riding the two horses through the dark over the frozen December ruts of that Christmas Eve: four of them and then just two—Charles-Shreve and Quentin-Henry" (267). By depicting the listener's inclusion in the story and demonstrating that listeners in oral storytelling are interchangeable with tellers, the text portrays the role that the reader plays when confronted with the various inconclusive narratives in the novel, forcing the reader to join the storytelling performance. That storytelling is a performance is highlighted by the inclusion of the listener. Shreve's comment, "Let me play," suggests not only the listener's ability to help construct the narrative but also the narrative's context of "play" or performance.

The inclusion of the audience in the performance is also evident when Quentin and Shreve perform or reenact an earlier storytelling performance from the narrative they are telling, a kind of doubled framing of the story, when Quentin tells Shreve the story of Sutpen telling General Compson about the riot in Haiti. Quentin explains that Sutpen told General Compson that "he went out and subdued them, and when he returned he and the girl became engaged to marry" (204). General Compson reacts with "but you didn't even know her; you told me that when the siege began you didn't even know her name" (204). Sutpen tells him, "It took me some time to recover," but as Quentin explains that does not answer Compson's questions about how he subdued the slaves and became engaged. Quentin says, "When he recovered he and the girl were engaged. Then he stopped" (205). Shreve does not understand and says, "All right. Go on." Quentin responds, "I said he stopped." Shreve, still not understanding, says, "I heard you. Stopped what?" and asks a string of questions very like the ones General Compson asks Sutpen. Quentin tells him, "He stopped talking, telling it" (205). In reenacting the earlier storytelling session between Compson and Sutpen, Quentin performs Sutpen's part by stopping his narrative of Sutpen's story when Sutpen stops telling the narrative. Shreve unknowingly performs Compson's part by asking about parts of the narrative he does not understand. The characters engage in a performance by the very telling of the story since the story is part of oral tradition, which exists only through reenactments of the initial performance. With the remaining gaps in the narrative, the text also includes the reader as part of the storytelling performance. In "playing" along with the narrator/author, the listener/reader is both constructing the story and performing the storytelling.

The reader of *Their Eyes Were Watching God* must bridge some gaps as well, the most glaring being the problem of the character of Tea Cake. In Janie's story to Pheoby, Tea Cake is the romantic hero. After her stifling marriages to Logan and Joe, Janie sees Tea Cake as love, escape, and freedom. Even when Tea Cake shows poor judgment, such as taking her money and throwing a party with it, she forgives him. Although she has to kill him in self-defense, she then thanks him "for giving her the chance for loving service" (184). Janie's many expressions of her love for Tea Cake—"he was a glance from God" (106), "her soul crawled out from its hiding place" (128), "Ah jus' know dat God snatched me out de fire through you" (180)—easily lull the reader of the novel into this version as well. But the narrator gives the reader opportunities to see a different picture of this relationship, particularly in the chapter where Tea Cake beats Janie to show Mrs. Turner and her brother that he has possession of Janie. Since the chapter is narrated entirely in voices other than Janie's, we can infer that this episode is not part of her story to Pheoby but is included by the narrator to show another view of their relationship. Several critics argue that Tea Cake is in fact no better than Janie's first two husbands. Thomas Cassidy, for example, argues that "in the story which she tells Pheoby, Janie tries to present her marriage to Tea Cake as the answer to the questions posed by her first two marriages and as a relationship based on love, equality, and mutual respect. The reader, however, sees a relationship filled with violence, thievery, and no small amount of jealousy" (260). Janie's marriage to Tea Cake is then in pattern with the first two marriages. To see this second version of Tea Cake, however, the reader must disagree with Janie's interpretation of her own life.[23] The reader can only do this if he or she has a role in determining the meaning. In replicating oral storytelling and splitting the narrative voice so the reader experiences Janie's story to Pheoby and the narrator's story to the audience of the novel, Hurston allows the reader to become like a listener to storytelling, an active participant in the narrative.

***

We must still, however, wonder why Hurston and Faulkner do this. Why develop these complex forms to include the reader? It cannot just be an attempt to celebrate folk culture in a time period that valued it. And although the reader's inclusion works well to further decentralize power, the other characters in the texts pretty well disrupt the containment needed by the master narrative of paradise. I would argue that the inclusion of the reader is essential because the reader has a specific job to do in these two novels. The reader must find the elusive matter of race at the heart of the narratives. Both texts deflect the issue of race and put off attention to it as much as possible to the very end, but both narratives turn on the problem of miscegenation and the reader is given the task of discovering the mixed blood.

Quentin and Shreve do discover the mixed blood of Charles Bon but not until the end of *Absalom, Absalom!* Their reconstruction of the conversation between Thomas Sutpen and Henry at a camp during the Civil War is the first time in the text that the "truth" (if this version is true) of Charles's parentage is known. They imagine that Henry proclaims to his father: "*Yes. I have decided. Brother or not, I have decided. I will. I will*" (283). It is only then that Sutpen tells Henry, "*It was not until after he was born that I found out that his mother was part negro*" (283). In this version Charles has known this all along, so that when Henry returns to his tent and tells Charles, "*You are my brother,*" Charles admits, "*No I'm not. I'm the nigger that's going to sleep with your sister*" (286). By keeping this vital piece of information away from the reader and out of the narrators' constructions about Bon until the end, the idea of Charles's mixed blood acts like the "snapper" that Mark Twain explains lies at the end of a good story. It surprises the audience and reverses the entire direction of the narrative. Quentin and Shreve arrive at this dramatic moment because Charles Bon's race trumps the earlier possible problems: bigamy because of his marriage to the octoroon or incest if he is Sutpen's son. In proclaiming, "*Brother or not,*" Henry suggests that he will go along with incest, but miscegenation is the final straw. If we have been sitting at the narrative version of a card game, the last hand holds all the aces.

The revelation of black blood, however, should not be a complete surprise to the careful reader; there have been hints all along that something is amiss. When Mr. Compson tries to craft the story around the problem of bigamy, he admits that it is not enough to warrant Henry's decision to kill Charles and keeps claiming, "It just does not explain" (80). When Quentin and Shreve decide that Charles is Sutpen's son and the problem is incest, they still cannot work out a narrative that makes sense. Shreve tries to suggest that Charles's insistence on marrying Judith was a way of getting his father to acknowledge him, but Quentin keeps interjecting that it does not add up. The reader keeps getting information on what was not the problem, which leads to the inevitable question of what the problem could be. Toni Morrison explains, "Faulkner in *Absalom, Absalom!* spends the entire book tracing race, and you can't find it. No one can see it, even the character who *is* black can't see it" ("Art" 101). Because race is hinted at but not revealed, the reader must do the work of finding it; Morrison says, "As a reader you have been forced to hunt for a drop of black blood that means everything and nothing. The insanity of racism. So the structure is the argument. Not what this one says, or that one says. . . . It is the *structure* of the book, and you are there hunting this black thing that is nowhere to be found, and yet makes all the difference" ("Art" 101). The "structure" that causes the reader to enter the text and hunt for race, I would argue, is oral storytelling. The written text is not fixed, not complete, so that the reader must act his or her part in the performance and find the absence at the center of the text.

That absence is embodied by Charles Bon, if indeed Charles Bon can be said to have a body. The first description of Charles in the text sets the tone for his mysterious existence; Mr. Compson speculates that he "must have appeared almost phoenix-like, full-sprung from no childhood, born of no woman and impervious to time and, vanished leaving no bones nor dust anywhere" (58). Rosa questions whether he left a body when she explains, "*I never saw him. I never even saw him dead*" (123). Although she helps bury the coffin, she can only trust Judith that Charles's body was in it: "*Yes, more than that: he was absent, and he was; he returned, and he was not; three women put something into the earth and covered it, and he had never been*" (123). He remains throughout the various characters' stories more specter than person, as Mr. Compson says, "Yes, shadowy: a myth, a phantom: Something which they engendered and created whole themselves; some effluvium of Sutpen blood and characters, as though as a man he did not exist at all" (82). Philip Weinstein, in speaking of Charles Bon's incomplete identity, explains, "Charles Bon enters this novel dead, is brought back to life, is shot, is resurrected, is shot again, is resurrected again, is shot again. Each time he dies it hurts a bit more, hurts Quentin and Shreve who have lent him something of themselves, hurts the reader who has lent Quentin and Shreve (and therefore Charles) something of the reader's self" (184). In examining the implications of Bon's lack of identity, Weinstein includes the reader in the process; the reader tries to identify with Charles and feels the absence.

In whatever manner the characters and the reader identify Charles and ponder his absence, his presence threatens the containment of paradise. Whether he is introducing bigamy, incest, or miscegenation into the Sutpen dynasty, the perfect design is in peril.[24] The worst danger would be miscegenation, as Charles himself understands when he says to Henry, "*So it's the miscegenation, not the incest, which you cant bear*" (285). It is this danger that Shreve taunts Quentin with at the end of the novel when he comments that there is "one nigger Sutpen left," Jim Bond, and that "in time the Jim Bonds are going to conquer the western hemisphere. Of course it wont quite be in our time and of course as they spread toward the poles they will bleach out again like the rabbits and the birds do, so they wont show up so sharp against the snow. But it will still be Jim Bond; and so in a few thousand years, I who regard you will also have sprung from the loins of African kings" (302). Shreve imagines a future of miscegenation stemming from the line of mixed-race progeny of Thomas Sutpen. Sutpen's white children, Judith and Henry, have no children and so the Sutpen legacy lives on only through Charles Bon's grandson, Jim Bond. Jim Bond will "conquer the western hemisphere" but only through further miscegenation, further racial mixing, so that they will, in Shreve's crude terms, "bleach out again." The novel's key threat is not the violence of civil war or fratricide but the possibility of miscegenation.

It is the reader who decides if this threat is real (and if we would term it a threat in the first place) because the reader must decide who Charles Bon is: is he the son, the brother, black, white, mixed, real, ghost? The oral story-telling that lets the reader into the narrative also leaves open the space for the reader to plug in an answer for Bon. We are not given carte blanche here though; the explanation that Eulalia Bon had some black blood and that Charles is her son by Thomas Sutpen and that Henry kills Charles to stop him from marrying his sister is obviously the most reasonable one presented by the narrators in the book.[25] We should ask, however, *why* it is the most reasonable; what is the rationality underlying Sutpen's racism and desire to construct a white paradise and why is the reader left to find race. Morrison describes the reader's role aptly as a "hunt" for black blood. It is a hunt because we are looking for a runaway slave. Early in the novel the hunt for the architect provides a kind of parody for the pursuit of a slave because the stakes are low. The architect is not harmed, is not in fact a slave, and gives up when found. But the hunt for the black blood in Charles Bon not only leads to murder, it makes the reader into a hunter. If the reader agrees with Quentin and Shreve's explanation of events, the reader must decide that miscegenation is the most rational reason for murder.[26] Quentin ends the novel in a panic claiming he does not hate the South and then in *The Sound and the Fury* commits suicide.

Another option, however, exists for the reader, who does not have to stay within Sutpen's flawed vision of paradise, where Charles Bon plays the racial threat. Because oral storytelling is ongoing with the narrative always subject to revision, the reader is free to modify the story. Quentin's vision of story-telling works well as a metaphor for this trajectory: "*Maybe nothing ever happens once and is finished. Maybe happen is never once but like ripples maybe on water after the pebble sinks, the ripples moving on, spreading, the pool attached by a narrow umbilical water-cord to the next pool which the first pool feeds, has fed, did feed, let this second pool contain a different temperature of water, a different molecularity of having seen, felt, remembered, reflect in a different tone the infinite unchanging sky*" (210). Shreve survives the story, "now a practicing surgeon, Edmonton,

Alta," indicating the ongoing nature of oral storytelling. In fact in his taunt to Quentin about Jim Bond, Shreve actually imagines himself in the future as mixed, "I who regard you will also have sprung from the loins of African kings"; that future is the ultimate destruction of Sutpen's racially pure paradise but is not the end of the story.

Their Eyes Were Watching God also seemingly deflects the reader's attention away from race until the last few chapters. The text focuses instead on gender differences as Janie tries to find romantic love. In the opening passage the narrator draws a distinction between the perspective of men, "ships at a distance have every man's wish on board," and the perspective of women, "women forget all those things they don't want to remember, and remember everything they don't want to forget" (1). The men and women watch as Janie returns to her house in Eatonville; while the men notice her appealing body, the women notice her dirty overalls. What matters is gender. When Janie sets out to tell her life story to Pheoby, she does not emphasize the impact of race in her childhood, although she tells the stories of living in the white family's household and not knowing until she sees a photograph of herself that she is black. While these could be key episodes in her formation, she picks instead the scene under the pear tree as her moment of maturity. Janie watches the "pear tree soaking in the alto chant of the visiting bees, the gold of the sun and the panting breath of the breeze when the inaudible voice of it all came to her. She saw a dust-bearing bee sink into the sanctum of a bloom; the thousand sister-calyxes arch to meet the love embrace and the ecstatic shiver of the tree from root to tiniest branch creaming in every blossom and frothing with delight" (11). She concludes, "So this was a marriage!" (11). With this natural and overly romantic view of love, Janie then sets out to find a man to match her vision. When Logan fails to meet her expectations, Janie complains to Nanny, "Ah wants things sweet wid mah marriage lak when you sit under a pear tree and think" (24). When Joe belittles her, she realizes "she wasn't petal-open anymore with him" (71). Tea Cake, however, comes closer to the vision: "He could be a bee to a blossom—a pear tree blossom in the spring" (106). Janie's constructs her story to Pheoby as a love story with gender not race playing a vital role.

Just as in Faulkner's novel, however, we are given hints of the effect of Janie's mixed race on the events. Nanny tells the story of having to escape the plantation shortly after giving birth to Janie's mother, Leafy, because the white mistress threatened to have her whipped for giving birth to a baby with gray eyes and yellow hair. Leafy is raped by a white schoolteacher, which results in her giving birth to Janie, making Janie what would be termed at the time "mulatto" or mixed race. Although she has more white grandparents than African American ones, the one-drop rule makes even the mulatto assigned wholly to the black race. Janie's light skin and long hair, however, play no small role in attracting the various husbands. Logan obviously marries her for her beauty since, as he points out, "Youse born in a carriage 'thout no top to it" (30). Joe also seems to relish her looks, forcing her to wear a head rag when he spies another man attempting to touch Janie's long hair. Even Tea Cake early in their courtship shows up at Janie's house with a comb for her hair because he "come prepared tuh lay mah hands on it tuhnight" (103). Hidden under Janie's story of love is the evident attraction of her long hair, a sign of that mixed heritage.

Her light skin also plays into her attraction for Mrs. Turner and into Mrs. Turner's efforts to get Janie to leave Tea Cake and marry her brother. The character of Mrs. Turner does introduce the subject of race, but her views on race are so ridiculous that they in effect deflate the importance of race. Mrs. Turner seeks Janie out specifically because of Janie's "coffee-and-cream complexion and her luxurious hair" (140). Mrs. Turner is mulatto herself, although not as light as Janie, and is mystified by Janie's attraction to Tea Cake. She thinks that mulattos should "class off" (141). Although Janie tries to discourage Mrs. Turner after Tea Cake discovers them talking bad about him, she is largely unsuccessful because, as the narrator explains, Mrs. Turner felt that "anyone who looked more white folkish than herself was better than she was in her criteria, therefore it was right that they should be cruel to her at times, just as she was cruel to those more negroid than herself in direct ratio to their negroness. Like the pecking order in a chicken yard" (144). Her distinctions based on shades of skin color combined with her hysteria about trying to escape from her race make her look silly, as Tea Cake at one point tells her, "Aw, don't make God look so foolish—findin' fault wid everything He made" (145).

Given the inattention to race by Janie and the deflation of race by the inclusion of a fool like Mrs. Turner, the trial scene comes as a shock. After Janie shoots Tea Cake in self-defense because he has gone mad with rabies, she is put on trial for murder. She is tried by an all-white jury with the black crowd from the muck standing at the back of the courtroom, "packed tight like a case of celery, only much darker than that," silenced by the judge but wanting to convict Janie because they assume she "took up with another man," namely Mrs. Turner's mulatto brother. Suddenly the race lines are drawn dramatically and the stakes could not be higher. Janie still thinks primarily in terms of gender when she comments that "twelve strange men who didn't know a thing about people like Tea Cake and her were going to sit on the thing" (185). Although we might initially read her statement as equating the lack of knowledge with the racial difference, when Janie sees the white women at the trial, she thinks, "It would be nice if she could make *them* know how it was instead of those menfolks" (185). Janie's attempt to draw gendered lines fails, however, because those white women are mere spectators and the power resides with the white men, particularly the "strange man from Palm Beach who was going to ask them not to kill her" (185). Although the black men standing at the back of the room are rendered powerless by the segregation of the legal system, Janie still feels threatened by their force: "So many were there against her that a light slap from each one of them would have beat her to death. She felt them pelting her with dirty thoughts. They were there with their tongues cocked and loaded, the only real weapon left to weak folks. The only killing tool they are allowed to use in the presence of white folks" (185–86). Ironically, however, they are not allowed this tool, as they are not allowed by the court to speak. The room remains divided strictly by race, with the "white part of the room" calm and serious and the "Negroes like wind among palm trees" (186). Janie is left in the middle.

The trial itself is nothing less than odd. Laura Korobkin analyzes the trial scene and finds that although the narrative sets up a justification of self-defense, this explanation is not even mentioned in the trial; the reason, Korobkin argues, is race. Korobkin looks at the various different constituents at the trial and examines their differing perspectives. The African American community wants to convict Janie because they think she was cheating on Tea Cake and "hanging was too good" for her (*Their Eyes* 186). When Janie gives her own testimony, she does not assert her right to defend herself but instead "implies that she shot Tea Cake to help him" (Korobkin 16). The judge then calls Janie a "poor broken creature" and, as Korobkin explains, "characterizes Janie's act as a mercy killing" (18). The jury comes back with the verdict of innocence because they find the shooting "accidental" (*Their Eyes* 188). Every single explanation is "counterfactual," Korobkin argues, and every perspective ignores Janie's own agency in choosing to save her life and shoot Tea Cake; she was not trying to rid herself of her husband to marry another, she was not choosing to put Tea Cake out of his misery, and the gun she was holding did not go off accidentally. She pulls the trigger to save herself. Korobkin argues, "Precisely because the theory of self-defense makes lethal violence rightful and universally available under certain circumstances, every empowered white person in the courtroom shies away from acknowledging or authorizing a black woman's recourse to violence" (18). Admitting Janie's right to defend herself, then, would give her too much agency as a black woman, but the black men still suspect her light skin was enough to prompt the white jury to find another reason to release her: "Aw you know dem white mens wuzn't gointuh do nothin' tuh no woman dat look lak her" (*Their Eyes* 189). In the end Janie's mixed race is crucial.

Janie, however, remains blind to its significance and continues to shape the story as a drama about love. She focuses on how Tea Cake got rabies by saving her from the mad dog and so "had to die for loving her" (178). She worries during the trial if the undertaker is "fixing Tea Cake up fine" (185). Janie's story at the trial particularly bothers critics who complain about the split in perspective because it is told completely in third person by the narrator. The reader even gets a hint that no one in the courtroom hears her because she is finished some time "before the judge and the lawyer and the rest seemed to know it" (187–88). I would again argue that the scene is in third person because it is not part of Janie's story to Pheoby; it is part of the narrator's story to the audience. Because Janie does not pay attention to the racial lines in the trial scene, the reader is given the job of finding the magnitude of race. If we put the trial in context, we can see race underlying all the events. Tea Cake and Janie do not leave the muck when the hurricane is approaching because Tea Cake trusts too much in the white man's power. Lias tries to warn Tea Cake about the approaching danger, but Tea Cake responds, "De white folks ain't gone nowhere. Dey oughta know if it's dangerous" (156). When Tea Cake and Janie get caught in the storm, they seek the higher ground of the bridge at Six Mile Bend. They end up in the river with the rabid dog because they are not allowed on the bridge: "White people had preempted that point of elevation and there was no more room" (164). The bridge serves as an apt symbol that, despite Janie's vision of romantic love, race becomes a dividing line. Janie may come back to Eatonville triumphant that she had "done been tuh de horizon and back," but the reader has to pay attention to the clues that Janie's story overlooks and find that the key factor in Janie's trial and Tea Cake's death is in fact race.

***

The desire to create racially pure paradises ends in narratives mired in the problems created by the attempt to draw lines based on race. Both *Their Eyes Were Watching God* and *Absalom, Absalom!* use oral storytelling to upset stabilized power, both display a tension between the words fixed on the page and the oral story that seems to walk off the page, yet Hurston and Faulkner write out of two different oral traditions—or do they? Joel Chandler Harris and Charles Chesnutt write narratives that are already mixed in their heritage. Whether Faulkner and Hurston draw off this mixed heritage, however, is hard to know for certain. David Minter explains that William Faulkner's education in oral storytelling came from various sources: "At the stove in his father's office he watched and listened as his father's friends drank whiskey and swapped tales. At the courthouse he listened to old men tell stories about the War. At the fireplace in Mammy Caroline Barr's cabin he found another place to listen. Born into slavery in 1840, Mammy Callie, as the Falkner boys called her, was more than sixty years old when the Murry Falkners moved to Oxford. . . . Unable to read or write, she remembered scores of stories about the old days and the old people: about slavery, the War, the Klan, and the Falkners" (12–13). Judith Sensibar digs further into Faulkner's relationship to Caroline Barr and argues that, "in his imagination, where Faulkner really lived, Callie Barr commanded lots of space" (21). Between Barr's influence and that of the "old men" Minter notes, Faulkner was surrounded by storytellers of both races.[27] Hurston's heritage obviously derives from her African American roots, and she details her exposure to great African American storytellers in *Mules and Men*, but her study of the discipline of anthropology and her use of the frame device suggest that there may be some influence from Western culture in at least how she chose to turn the oral storytelling into a written form. Although I cannot parse the subjective question of exactly who was influenced by whom or what, both Faulkner and Hurston responded to their historical context with their interest in folk culture, and there is surely confluence in how they both tackle the problem of paradise, how they both use oral storytelling, and how they both step gingerly around the bomb of race and leave it still ticking for the reader to find. That bomb will explode in the following chapter with the next two modern writers, Welty and Ellison.

3
Getting the Last Laugh

Ralph Ellison's *Invisible Man* and
Eudora Welty's *Losing Battles*

On May 6, 1935, President Franklin Delano Roosevelt signed an executive order creating the Works Progress Administration (WPA); in July of that same year, the Federal Writers' Project (FWP) was born as a branch of the WPA. Monty Penkower explains in his history of the FWP that it was "never intended as a subsidized cultural enterprise" but was instead "established to provide work relief for writers and other white-collar personnel caught in the toils of the Depression" (238). By the time it ended seven years later, however, the FWP was the "biggest literary project in history," having spent a little over $27 million and resulting in "enough material to fill seven twelve-foot shelves in the library of the Department of the Interior" (237).

The effects of the government sponsorship of the arts ended up going far beyond economic relief. Although the FWP projects were designed to document American culture in the 1930s, they also helped to construct that culture, particularly the regard for regionalism. The "America" depicted on those shelves of documents is diverse, but many of the WPA and FWP projects particularly emphasized the value of regional cultures. Christine Bold explains the larger theory behind this focus: "Regionalism was a key word for intellectuals in the 1930s, combining a belief in the vitality of modern folk art with a conviction that landscape could be translated into culture; the diverse physical resources of the country, went the argument, inescapably gave rise to diverse forms of cultural expression. Therein lay America's true richness and its full independence from Europe" (31). America was its many regions, and in a country crippled by an economic depression, folk culture surfaced as a distinctive and thus valuable American cultural resource. The WPA and FWP tapped into this resource by documenting the varieties of folk cultures. Artists and writers paid to do the documenting then found rich material for their own works.

Ralph Ellison and Eudora Welty were two such writers. Although Ellison published *Invisible Man* in 1952 and Welty published *Losing Battles* in 1970, both writers set the plots of their novels in the 1930s and draw from their experiences working for the WPA to depict this time period. From 1938 to 1942, Ellison worked for the FWP collecting folklore in New York City. He interviewed many older people, asking them to tell him stories and tall tales. He also hung around playgrounds recording children's jokes, rhymes, and games.[1] Welty worked for the WPA from 1933 to 1936 as a "junior publicity agent." She traveled all over Mississippi writing newspaper copy and taking photographs of people and scenes in rural areas.[2] The job exposed her to the plight of poor Mississippians during the Depression.

Welty's and Ellison's experiences put them in the company of many other writers, such as Zora Neale Hurston, Margaret Walker, Langston Hughes, and Richard Wright, who all worked in one capacity or another for the WPA, and they are not alone in putting their WPA experience to good use by incorporating it into their work. The influence may go deeper, however. When Ellison and Welty employ this material in their own literary works, they depict the older folk culture, particularly oral storytelling, as valuable and powerful. This positive depiction aligns with the culture of the WPA. Although the storytellers in both books are poor people seemingly left behind by the modern world, they are not fading peacefully, and certainly not quietly, away into the history books.

The "folk" that modifies "culture" is admittedly very different in the two novels. Ellison's unnamed narrator confronts the folk culture of African Americans who, although transplanted to New York City, bring their older southern traditions and stories with them. Because I am examining this older southern tradition, I include *Invisible Man*, with its southern content, in this study, even though whether Ellison himself would be considered southern is debatable. Despite the narrative's southern roots, Ellison's novel would seem to have nothing in common with Eudora Welty's novel chronicling the story of a large rural white family's reunion in Depression-era Mississippi. It is in fact the vast difference in subject matter that makes these novels an interesting pair.[3] Ellison's narrator finds himself presented with a cacophony of dissonant voices, but they line up roughly into two camps: those for a folk culture that values oral storytelling and African American history versus those for a modern culture that values scientific discourse and a raceless view of the future. The narrator can think of the world as wholly segregated by race or as wholly uninformed by race, but in either scenario, his identity is constructed by the political situation of segregation. Welty's novel, on the other hand, includes not a single African American character. The members of the Beecham-Renfro family do not acknowledge segregation as a problem;

they are too worried about surviving a drought and a depression. Welty, however, is certainly cognizant that this world is segregated. One of the characters, Uncle Nathan, explains his decision to wander the world by admitting that years before he "killed Mr. Dearman with a stone to his head, and let 'em hang a sawmill nigger for it" (344). The novel does not explore why this character killed Mr. Dearman, who "'em" were, or who the tragic victim of the lynching was, but this one brief statement points to the ugly racial reality of this world.[4] The family does not want to tell the rest of this particular story. Their storytelling is instead an attempt to maintain the status quo, the comfortable white world they know. The storytelling by Ellison's characters draws race lines as well because only insiders, which in this novel are black rural folk, understand the stories. In both books, storytelling seems to support segregation.

The oral traditions these characters draw from to tell their stories are not, however, segregated. The oral storytelling in *Losing Battles* and *Invisible Man* is mixed, the cultural traditions entangled and intertwined. Ellison points to the influence of white writers on his use of folklore, and the storytelling in the novel shows evidence of both white and African American sources. Welty's other work shows traces of influence from African American sources that may shed some light on her debt to African American cultural traditions in *Losing Battles*. Ellison and Welty both draw from the tall tale tradition, from popular culture and the cinema, from African American signifying, and even from Joel Chandler Harris's wily Brer Rabbit.

More significant than the traces of confluence is the depiction in both books of the same strategy in the oral storytelling: the stories become weapons as the humor in the stories is subversive. Critics have dismissed the humor in both books as window dressing that readers should bypass to get to the serious import of the novels' explorations of race and class, but I will argue in this chapter for a reading of the laughter as a credible force. The humor in these texts works much the same way as it does in Harris's and Chesnutt's works in forming communities. Here, however, those communities are embattled and the folk are losing their way of life, so the humor becomes a way of fighting back. Glenda Carpio in analyzing the use of humor in fictions about slavery explains that "African American humor, like other humor that arises from oppression, has provided a balm, a release of anger and aggression, a way of coping with the painful consequences of racism" (5). She then argues that this literature fulfills Freud's explanation of laughter as aggressive, as a way to release hostilities. Ellison's narrator certainly uses laughter as a mask for the aggression he feels because of his invisible status, as does the family in Welty's novel, whose poverty of resources and education is highlighted by their interactions with outsiders. In both books the folk use their laughter to try to gain the power in words they lack in reality.

Laughter as a weapon connects these folk with the folk Mikhail Bakhtin writes about in describing carnivalistic laughter. Bakhtin explains the dynamics of carnival as a reversal of power structures, a "temporary liberation from the prevailing truth and from established order" (*Rabelais* 10). Carnivalistic laughter then is "directed toward a higher order—toward the change of authorities and truths, toward the change of world orders" (*Problems* 104). This laughter becomes in the folk's hands a "weapon" (*Rabelais* 94). The folk in the modern novels attempt to tap into this tradition of using humor to combat the stronger forces of "established order," and their aim is to wrest some amount of control. Bakhtin explains that in medieval carnival tradition the laughter was linked to rebirth and renewal, so that its motives are ambivalent: "It is gay, triumphant, and at the same time mocking, deriding. It asserts and denies, it buries and revives" (*Rabelais* 11–12). The folk in Ellison's and Welty's novels use their weapons primarily to mock and bury, and the second movement of revival may be missing, but ambivalence finds its way into the texts in another form.

The battles in both books are ongoing, so both novels end with ambivalence. Critics of *Invisible Man* often complain that the narrator's hibernation in his hole equals apathy. They want the direct approach of a protest novel instead. Critics of *Losing Battles* often rewrite the novel to settle the score, choosing a winner and thus ignoring the novel's own ambivalence about the value of each side. Oral storytelling might be a key factor in each novel's reluctance to take a side in the battles depicted. The same oral storytelling that comes from a confluence of cultures also leads to a valuing of the middle ground. Tellers and listeners must find a verbal space for interaction. The very ambivalence critics complain about is the goal of oral storytelling, a meeting in the middle to share the construction of a story. And while Welty and Ellison do not depict happy endings to the battles in their texts (we will have to wait for the next chapter for that possibility), they do refuse to place their sympathy wholly with either side. Modernism is winning the day in both novels, as the folk cultures are fading and the older traditions are dying, but with the folk using humor to undermine their opponents, they at least get the last laugh.

***

Although *Invisible Man* and *Losing Battles* both play out a struggle between the forces of traditional rural folk culture and a progressive urban modernism, the players in the battles are quite different. *Losing Battles* has a large cast of characters including the family matriarch, Granny Vaughn, all of Granny's descendants gathered for the reunion, and multiple visitors who end up at the Renfro house for various reasons during the reunion. The most notable visitor is Judge Moody, who not only sent the family's beloved Jack Renfro to prison but threatens their well-being once again by suggesting that Jack's marriage to Gloria is illegal if they are indeed proven to be first cousins. His wealth, education, and dedication to written evidence make him the epitome of an "outsider" to the family members, who are poor, uneducated, and dedicated to their own oral tradition. The battle lines are drawn.

To maneuver Judge Moody into attending the family's reunion, Welty writes a plot worthy of slapstick comedy. Jack "borrows" a ride home from jail by holding onto the judge's bumper and thus is in the perfect position to help the judge when he slides into a ditch. When Jack later discovers whom it was he helped, he sets back out on the road to revise his good deed and put the judge's car back into a ditch. Judge Moody's car instead ends up teetering at the top of a cliff, and Jack invites Judge Moody to the reunion. While this is all in good fun, Welty is actually drawing on her WPA experience to imagine a scene where the folk culture and the modern culture could meet. As Welty drove around rural Mississippi, she was the urban outsider learning about folk culture. Welty points to this experience as the genesis of her decision to become a writer: "In my own case, a fuller awareness of what I needed to find out about people and their lives had to be sought for through another way, through writing stories. But away off one day up on Tishomingo County, I knew this anyway: that my wish, indeed my continuing passion, would be not to point the finger in judgment but to part a curtain, that invisible shadow that falls between people, the veil of indifference to each other's presence, each other's wonder, each other's human plight" (*One Time* 12). She places the beginning of her writing career in Tishomingo County, the setting she later uses for *Losing Battles*. Welty links the WPA trips and the novel itself: "But just when I was working on *Losing Battles*, a novel set in that part of the world, so much came back to me of what I had absorbed" ("Eudora" 192).

Putting the modern American in touch with folk culture was in fact one of the goals of the WPA. The main task of the Federal Writers' Project was the American Guide series, which was a collection of guidebooks, one for each state. The rationale was that "without decent guidebooks, Americans sped through towns, and past scenery on the best highways in the world, unaware of the rich variety of their history and folklore" (Penkower 25). The claim of the American Guide series publicists was "Americans Discover America" (Bold 5). In driving a car through rural Mississippi, Judge Moody is the perfect candidate for the Mississippi guide, which targeted the casual tourist. Although Welty did not work directly on the Mississippi guide, three of her photographs appeared in the 1938 publication (Waldron 74). The Mississippi guide's description of the area where *Losing Battles* is set accurately depicts the opinion the judge has toward the scene outside his car window: "The cedar and pine forests are more depleted, the shacks more dilapidated, the people fewer, and the crops poorer, because of the sterility of the sandy red soil. Here and there is a two- or three-room shack of old, unpainted wood, with a tin roof, a dog-trot through the center, a mud chimney, and a slack line across the porch for faded garments. The people often go barefooted and many are listless in manner" (446). The guide seems to struggle at making the poverty picturesque. Christine Bold explains that the point of view in the guides is that of the driver passing by the scenery; the interesting folk culture was "out there, in the surrounding landscape" distanced from the guidebook user (8). The problem, of course, for Judge Moody, is that he does not get to remain secluded in his car. Instead of whizzing past the landscape, the judge ends up lost in the middle of it, which he describes in language reminiscent of the guidebook, as the very "pocket of ignorance" (*Losing Battles* 304). By wrecking the car, Welty puts the older rural folk culture in direct conversation with the outside, the "American" gets to see "America."

Ralph Ellison also uses an automobile to drive the modern back into the past when the narrator takes Mr. Norton on a ride in the country. Mr. Norton is a white benefactor of the narrator's college; the narrator's pithy description pegs Mr. Norton as a believer in progress: "shrewd banker, skilled scientist, director, philanthropist" (*Invisible Man* 37). Mr. Norton tells the narrator that he has put his money into the college as a kind of monument for his deceased daughter, hoping that by funding the education of young students like the narrator, he is making the future better: "You are bound to a great dream and to a beautiful monument" (43). When the narrator, lost in contemplating the white man's lofty hopes for him, turns down a dirt road, Norton expresses his surprise at the scenery: "Is that a *log* cabin?" (46). He is simply aghast when the narrator explains that the cabins are left over from the days of slavery. Modern progress then meets folk culture as Norton asks the narrator to stop the car so he can meet the man so vile, or backward, that he impregnated both his wife and daughter at the same time. Mr. Norton gets more than he bargained for when he hears the storytelling of Jim Trueblood, and the narrator is horrified: "How all of us at the college hated the black-belt people, the 'peasants,' during those days! We were trying to lift them up and they, like Trueblood, did everything it seemed to pull us down" (47).

This trip into the countryside gets the narrator kicked out of school and sends him to New York to seek a job while supposedly waiting to reenter his beloved college. While in New York, however, the narrator keeps getting reminders of his childhood in the South, either through his own memories or through conversations such as the one he has with a street vendor selling sweet potatoes. At times, he shows nostalgia for the remnants of the older folk traditions, but he also tries to separate himself from those embracing the African American cultural traditions because he believes in the raceless future promised by the Brotherhood. When, for example, the waiter in a diner offers him the "special" of the day, a dinner of pork chops and grits, the narrator is embarrassed and wonders, "Could everyone see that I was southern?" (178). His relationship with his landlady, Mary Rambo, is fraught with this tension. Ellison actually drew from his WPA experience to create the character of Mary, who is a proponent of the older tradition though now transplanted to the North. In a collection on the WPA, Ann Banks includes Ellison's interview with Lloyd Green, in which Green utters the lines Ellison later puts in Mary's mouth, "I'm in New York, but New York ain't in me" (Banks 250). Although the narrator is indebted to Mary's care and is comforted by her down-home hospitality and cooking, he resists the connection back to southern folk culture. He is, for example, enraged when he sees that Mary owns a bank that figures a "very black, red-lipped and wide-mouthed Negro, whose white eyes stared up at me from the floor, his face an enormous grin, his single large black hand held palm up before his chest" (*Invisible Man* 319). The bank reflects the minstrel tradition with its exaggerated African features. The narrator tries to break it, but it is made of iron. He then tries twice to throw it away but is thwarted at every turn. A woman gets mad that he is using her trash can, saying that he is one of the "field niggers coming up from the South and ruining things." Then a man accuses him of working a con by dropping the bank in the street. The narrator gives up and puts the bank in his briefcase. The fight between the older culture and the new in this novel is within the psyche of the narrator as he literally carries around the burden of the past.

***

In both novels, the folk culture is clearly losing the battle; the forces of modernism are too much for people wanting to tell stories in the face of dramatic change. In *Invisible Man* the doom is evident in the eviction scene. When the narrator happens upon the eviction of two elderly African Americans from their home, he is startled that they could just be turned out on the street. Although he wants to ignore the tragic situation, he feels himself "drawn to the old couple by a warm, dark, rising whirlpool of emotion which I feared" (270). He attempts to remain detached from the couple but fails; when he sees a photograph of them as a young couple, he begins "feeling strange memories awakening that began an echoing in my head like that of a hysterical voice stuttering in a dark street" (271). The echoing voice connects him with another young man, Quentin Compson, who likewise cannot shake the past. In trying to make sense of the scene and to avoid eye contact with the people, the narrator examines their goods lying on the sidewalk. Many of the artifacts link the couple to older folk culture. The narrator sees "'knocking bones,' used to accompany music at country dances, used in black-face minstrels" (271). He sees "nuggets of High John the Conqueror," which according to tradition were lucky stones. The narrator begins to almost panic when he finds free papers, thinking, "*It has been longer than that, further removed in time*" (272). He wants to focus on the future and progress and is distressed when confronted by the past represented by the couple's belongings. As much as he feels tied to the couple, who bring up memories of his childhood and his mother, the narrator is also appalled that these people did not adapt to the modern world and that they have nothing to show for their labor: "Look at his old blues records and her pots of plants, they're down-home folks, and everything tossed like junk whirled eighty-seven years in a cyclone. Eighty-seven years and poof!" (278). The past is put out on the sidewalk.

The Beecham-Renfro family also seems to have little to show for their labor, and the older rural culture is clearly dying. At the reunion while the older generation tells the stories, the younger generation does not sit at their feet, soaking in the family history. With the exception of Beulah's children, all the other children and grandchildren remain at the margins of the text, playing a baseball game in the distance. While Gloria estimates to Judge Moody that the reunion crowd numbers about fifty, only a handful are involved in the oral storytelling. This pattern is indicative of the lives of the family members. Most of the children of this elder generation have moved away from their parents' rural farms; Uncle Curtis, for example, claims that they are all relying on Jack "since all my boys done up and left the farm" (*Losing Battles* 194). They have left because the farms can no longer provide a decent income. Uncle Dolphus explains, "It's the fault of the land going back on us, treating us the wrong way. There's been too much of the substance washed away to grow enough to eat any more. Now well's run dry and river's about to run dry" (194). One factor in the impoverishment of the land is the clear-cutting of trees. The family tells the story of Mr. Dearman, who "showed up full-grown around here, took over some of the country, brought niggers in here, cut down every tree within forty miles, and run it shrieking through a sawmill" (341). His maniacal drive puts him in line with Thomas Sutpen in his attempt to dominate nature for his own ends.[5] Instead of paying everyone for their trees, Dearman was a crafty enough businessman to have everyone owing him money by the time he completed the job. He even ended up owning Mr. Renfro's store and house, although Renfro does not know quite how that happened. Although Uncle Nathan killed Mr. Dearman, his ghost lives on in the stumps he left behind; the landscape still shows the wounds of his actions.

At the heart of modernism's superiority in both novels is the machine, both as a literal force and as a metaphor for the destructive potential of modernism's valuing of progress. In *Invisible Man* the narrator confronts a destructive machine when he tries to work at the paint factory. After learning that the paint factory puts black dope into their white paint to somehow make it whiter and then messing up a batch of paint himself by inserting the wrong "dope," the narrator gets sent to the basement. After going through three doors labeled "Danger," the narrator ends up in a metaphorical hell with its own version of Lucifer in the engineer, Lucius Brockaway. Brockaway claims to be the demon running the vast machinery of the plant, telling the narrator, "*We the machines inside the machines*" (217). Brockaway, however, is so paranoid about the union trying to take away his power that he attacks the narrator when the latter explains that he was delayed in getting his lunch because he ran into a union meeting in the locker room. Brockaway himself seems to be a figure from folk culture. The narrator at one point even thinks he looks like "Tar Baby," but the machine itself is the modern industrial complex in all its destructive potential. The character of Brockaway suggests that black labor is still at the heart of the complex. When the machine explodes, the narrator is caught in the basement, "[sprawling] in an interval of clarity beneath a pile of broken machinery, my head pressed back against a huge wheel, my body splattered with a stinking goo" (230).

In *Losing Battles'* rural setting, the most powerful machine in sight is the judge's Buick, and it too plays the role of a destructive force in the novel.[6] The car fits nicely into the American literary pattern identified by Leo Marx of the machine in the garden. Banner's rural and remote location, as Mrs. Moody says, a "long way off from everything," might render it a pastoral garden, untouched by the forces of modern technology (333). Jack and Gloria, waiting under the tree for Judge Moody's Buick to pass by, could even figuratively be Adam and Eve, at least until the preacher, Brother Bethune, kills the snake. Brother Bethune is wandering around Banner Top, having lost his mule and his bearings, because, as he explains, "a great big pleasure car in a cloud of dust and pine cones like to hit me right in the middle of the road" (107). The car again threatens to run over someone when Jack tries to scare the car into a second ditch. He and Gloria stumble, leaving the baby Lady May to "set forth across the road" right into the path of the car, which "came thundering for the top of the hill, a sunset of red dust fanning into high air, bank to bank" (120). Gloria manages to jump on top of the baby but still lies "flat there in the middle of Banner Road as if she waited in the path of a cyclone" (120). The car swerves, barely missing them, and charges up Banner Top, barely missing the tree in which Etolye is perched. As it comes to rest on nothing but Uncle Nathan's ominous sign, "Destruction Is At Hand," the engine is still running, as if, in Jack's words, "she's wondering if she can go ahead and fly" (123). Jack's reference to the car as "she" is apt, since the car seems to have become a character. As the Buick teeters in its most precarious position, it has one passenger left. In all the commotion, Jack's friend Aycock jumps in the backseat to provide ballast. If the car does indeed decide to fly, Aycock will go with it. Although no one is killed by the car in this scene, seven people are in harm's way, and with the car teetering on the edge of the cliff, the potential for danger is not over.

The other vehicles in the novel seem poised for menace as well. Jack's truck, for example, is now owned by his archnemesis Curly because the family could not pay for the new roof on their house without selling the truck. Jack acquired the former Coca-Cola truck in the first place because it was smashed by a second machine disturbing the garden, a train. Jack rebuilt the truck from pieces he salvaged from the creek bed below the train tracks. Even the school bus always seems slightly out of control in the story, careening itself from ditch to ditch and making it just one more time over the Banner bridge, which the family jokes is primed to collapse. The characters should realize the danger posed by the Buick, but they are too busy enjoying Jack's revenge. Miss Beulah is the exception, screaming, "These boys, these men, they don't realize anything! . . . What makes you think that's the end of the story? Somebody's still going to have to coax that car *down*. Suppose you never thought of that, any of you? What goes up has got to come down!" (199–200). Beulah is right to worry about how the car will get down. Mr. Renfro attempts to move the obstacle of the tree by blowing it up with dynamite. He walks with a limp from a previous accident with dynamite, and Aycock, who was still in the car, later admits to Beulah, "I feel like Mr.

Renfro kind of aimed to blow me up" (389). The Buick poses not just a literal danger to the characters in the novel but together with Dearman's sawmill proves how destructive modern forces can be.

***

The older oral culture, favored by the rural folk, appears to be losing in both novels, but the folk find a way to use their traditions to fight back. The proponents of progress armed with machines might be winning, but the folk employ their oral skills as a weapon. The folk use humor to subvert the serious business of progress. To see the humor as a weapon instead of just a diversion, however, is difficult. Critics of both books often bypass the jokes to get to the serious and apparently more valuable discussions about class and race but miss the subversion, admittedly subtle at times, enacted by proponents of folk culture. Responding to an interviewer who asked him a number of probing questions about his novel, Ellison asked, "Look, didn't you find the book at all *funny?*" (*Collected Essays* 221). Comedy is in fact the center stage in both books. Sharon Weinstein argues that *Invisible Man* "can be viewed as the protagonist's education in laughter" (12). She argues that the protagonist needs to see the absurdity of the world to find his place in it. Certainly the narrator must get the jokes if he is going to be an insider, someone with the ability to change the world, but Weinstein argues that the laughter must eventually be abandoned for real action; the narrator must "go beyond laughter" (13). The problem with her reading is twofold. The book stops before the "action" Weinstein wants to see, as the narrator in the epilogue plans to rejoin society but is still in his hole, and Weinstein is defining "action" so that the laughter itself is not an action, is not, in her words "constructive." If we, however, pay attention to how the characters use their humor, we can see it as a force, as a way of fighting back against the modern society that has, perhaps prematurely, claimed victory.

Ellison himself points to laughter in describing the genesis of his novel. When trying to write serious fiction about the search for identity, Ellison claims he was interrupted by a "taunting, disembodied voice," which he at first found annoying. He then changed his mind: "Given the persistence of racial violence and the unavailability of legal protection, I asked myself, what else *was* there to sustain our will to persevere but laughter? And could it be there was a subtle triumph hidden in such laughter that I had missed, but one which still was more affirmative than raw anger?" (*Invisible Man* xv–xvi). Those on the side of the folk culture use laughter against progressives such as Jack from the Brotherhood, who explains to the narrator, "I don't joke with you. Or play with words either" (307).

Peter Wheatstraw does joke with the narrator when the narrator meets him on the street one morning as Wheatstraw is pushing a cart loaded with blueprints. He is hauling the blueprints away for "the man" who apparently needed room for new plans. Wheatstraw is engaged in modern business; blueprints are a written record of urban planning. However, as he pushes the cart, he sings a song about a woman with "feet like a monkey" and makes jokes about a bear that has him from behind. Thinking that the narrator is a southern boy from "down home" who will understand the jokes, Wheatstraw shares the folklore. The narrator, however, makes the mistake of taking him literally, and when Wheatstraw asks him, "Is you got the dog?" the narrator looks around for a dog. While the narrator does not yet understand the jokes, the humor is actually Wheatstraw's defense. He downplays the importance of the blueprints as just somebody's plans that got changed and enjoys his own banter, "Damn if I'm-a let 'em run *me* into my grave" (175). He informs the narrator that "all it takes to get along in this here man's town is a little shit, grit, and mother-wit" and promises to teach him some "good bad habits" (176). His humor is his strength.

The family members in *Losing Battles* also use oral stories, jokes, and verbal play to fight back. They respond to the dangerous machine invading their garden by turning the judge's Buick into a big joke. When the Moodys and Jack and Gloria make it back to the reunion and tell the story, the family laughs and cheers. When Aunt Nanny asks if the car is indeed "out on the flirting edge of nowhere," she shakes with laughter. When Uncle Noah Webster hears that it is Gloria who caused the car to swerve off the road, he cries, "Bless your heart!" and kisses her, and Aunt Nanny adds, "Now that's what I call trying to make yourself a member of the family!" The family thinks that Banner Top is better than a ditch and glories at Jack's revenge. But their humor serves a deeper purpose as well. By choosing to laugh at the incident, they downplay both the immediate threat the car just posed to their beloved son Jack and his family and the larger threat of modernity crashing through the rural isolation they seem to cherish.

Judge Moody is an even more dangerous threat to the Beecham-Renfro family than his vehicle, so the family uses its oral skills to turn him comical as well. As Jack remarks, with the white handkerchief across his face, the judge "[looks] more like a bank robber than any judge" (82). He does threaten to rob the family of their much-needed son a second time. Jack admits to the family in the judge's hearing that he escaped from Parchman one day before his release so he could come to the reunion. The judge could send him back to jail or make a judgment about Jack and Gloria's questionable marriage. As they do with the car, the family tries to downplay the threat of Judge Moody by making fun of him. Brother Bethune starts the reunion off by claiming to the judge, "We're going to forgive you" (208). While Jack is appalled, the rest of the reunion quickly gets the joke and joins in. They forgive him in turn for wrecking his car, for bringing his wife, and for living, skirting around the real issue of why they are angry with him and having a rollicking good time in the process. The judge in the meantime is confused by the ceremony and hates being the butt of a joke he does not understand; he complains that they are "[making] a clown" of him. Jack finally explains to him that "they're trying to forgive you for sending me to the pen" (209), which causes Aunt Birdie then to announce he was forgiven for that too. Jack alone refuses to participate, which leads to the humorous ending of Jack and Moody shaking hands and agreeing that the judge should not be forgiven. The family is clearly having some fun at their guest's expense, but the humor effects the important work of overturning the vast power difference between Moody and the family, an attempt to create, in Bakhtin's words, a "change of world orders." By forgiving Judge Moody they suggest that they have the power usually ascribed to a deity to do the forgiving. If he needs forgiving, he is in the role of the penitent and without power.

***

Both novels, then, have characters, who despite the imminent demise of their cultural traditions, choose to laugh. Those cultural traditions may, however, in fact be related so that the impulses to fight back with laughter by both the rural white family in *Losing Battles* and the African Americans in *Invisible Man* might not be a coincidence, but evidence of some strains of shared culture. Ellison himself is the staunchest proponent for the influences of Western white culture on his own fiction, often citing Hemingway, Eliot, Joyce, and Twain as key influences. Critics have certainly examined Western influences in *Invisible Man* by discussing Freud or Joyce or Homer in connection to the narrator's quest for identity.[7] However, when critics examine the folklore sections of the novel, they speak solely of an African American influence.[8] Ellison himself would again point elsewhere: "I use folklore in my work not because I am Negro, but because writers like Eliot and Joyce made me conscious of the literary value of my folk inheritance. My cultural background, like that of most Americans, is dual (my middle name, sadly enough, is Waldo). I knew the trickster Ulysses just as early as I knew the wily rabbit of Negro American lore, and I could easily imagine myself a pint-sized Ulysses but hardly a rabbit, no matter how human and resourceful or Negro" (*Collected Essays* 112). Ellison's statement is interesting not just because he attributes his inclusion of folklore to the influence of white writers but because of the particular image, the trickster rabbit, he uses for African American lore. Despite the demurral, the rabbit does find his way into Ellison's novel in the scene in the factory hospital when the doctor asks the narrator, "Who was Brer Rabbit?" The narrator responds by using what little knowledge of folk tradition he has to play the dozens (a game of insults): "He was your mother's back-door man" (242). Although Brer Rabbit is a well-known trickster figure in African American folklore, he is best known in American literature through the writings and voice of the white writer, Joel Chandler Harris. The stories ricochet from the African American storytellers that Harris listened to as a boy, then back to Harris, and then to Ellison. The African American folk culture has both African and American roots. This might not be what everyone wants to hear. Susan Blake argues that, "What Ellison learned to do, in order to adapt black folk expression in literature, was to turn it into ritual and to put it at the service of a myth 'larger,' or other, than itself" (122). She complains that this larger Western myth acts to "distort, or deny the peculiarities of folk expression" (123). If we reverse the object and the field, however, to examine how the Western myth gets translated into the black folklore, the folk culture Ellison valued is not diminished but is portrayed as the mixture of the "peculiarities" of African American oral culture with the "peculiarities" of white oral culture. This does indeed work against the strict quest for distinctive black experience Blake wants to see, but what Ellison shows in *Invisible Man* is that the cultures are already mixed anyway.

Ellison argues that there is an "ironic obstacle which lies in the path of anyone who would fashion a theory of American Negro culture while ignoring the intricate network of connections which binds Negroes to the larger society. To do so is to attempt delicate brain surgery with a switchblade. And it is possible that any viable theory of Negro American culture obligates us to fashion a more adequate theory of American culture as a whole. The heel bone is, after all, connected through its various linkages to the head bone" (*Collected Essays* 283). Ellison argues here for a mixture of cultural influences, but he also claims that this mixture shapes more than the way African American culture is depicted in his work. All of American literature is affected; the particular stories do not then just plug into larger Western myths to make them accessible to a white reading public, they change those myths by their very inclusion. Alan Nadel discusses Ellison's "sense of integration" and explains that for Ellison, "just as white American music, dance, and humor are the composite of multiracial, multiethnic influences, so Negro American literature reflects the legacy of a literary tradition that is anything but monoracial" ("Integrated" 149).

Ellison's novel does not even keep a strict segregation of its influences. Characters who spout African American folklore in their oral storytelling performances also show threads of other influences. Peter Wheatstraw is the character that Timothy Spaulding reads as the "guiding voice as a representation of the black folk tradition" (490). In crafting oral jokes and verbal games to poke fun at the modern machinery of progress, Wheatstraw draws on African American folk traditions. He talks about a dog and a bear getting him from behind; the narrator with a surge of homesickness connects these images to childhood stories of Jack the Rabbit and Jack the Bear. Wheatstraw's fast talk is filled with verbal play: "My name is Peter Wheatstraw. I'm the Devil's only son-in-law, so roll 'em!" (176). He performs this folk culture, however, while wearing Charlie Chaplin pants, connecting him to yet a different comic tradition. Chaplin's trademark baggy pants were exaggerated for effect. In his autobiography, Chaplin recalls coming up with the outfit that would make him famous: "I wanted everything to be a contradiction: the pants baggy, the coat tight, the hat small and the shoes large" (154). The resulting haphazard look turned into Chaplin's best-known character, the tramp. According to David Weddle, Chaplin's tramp was "all id, an agent of anarchy in an age of social regimentation and economic segregation" (4). Wheatstraw in laughing at the powerbrokers who make and change plans also figures as an "agent of anarchy," singing his bizarre song about the woman with "feet like a monkey." In his baggy pants, shuffling along and pushing the cart, Wheatstraw plays the part of a tramp as well. Weddle explains that the attraction of Chaplin's tramp was that he provided a stark contrast to the "age of steel and the automobile" and "was a scrappy survivor who not only endured, but thrived" (4). Wheatstraw is not going to let "the man" get him down. Against the machinery of modernism, Wheatstraw uses his verbal prowess to show that he, too, is the "scrappy survivor." Chaplin's character may in fact be one layer under Ellison's portrayal of the battle between modern machinery and comic folklore. In Chaplin's 1936 movie, *Modern Times*, the tramp works in a factory on an assembly line. When he cannot keep up with his job of screwing nuts onto machinery, he has a mental breakdown and is sent to a hospital. After his recovery, he is arrested for participating in a Communist demonstration, although he becomes involved by mistake. The plotline of the narrator of *Invisible Man*—working in a factory, waking up in the factory hospital after an explosion, and getting out only to become involved in a protest at the eviction scene—roughly follows the plot of *Modern Times*. Whether the echo is intentional, the contrast of the comic character against the serious business of modern industry is the same. Wheatstraw wears Chaplin's pants in the novel because he becomes the id laughing back at the modern world.

By injecting a bit of Chaplin into Wheatstraw's character, Ellison is certainly linking Wheatstraw to a larger Western myth. Chaplin capitalized on a well-known figure in vaudeville that grew from the iconic image of the clown (Weddle 4). But Wheatstraw's act is also a parody of Chaplin, a parody of a parody in fact. If Chaplin's character parodies the pretensions of a modern world that believed in progress and took itself too seriously, Ellison ups the ante by making the tramp black, thereby adding the more highly visible segregation of race to the contrast provided by the character. That Ellison uses a character whose verbal skills are his weapon heightens the parody because Chaplin's character appeared in silent films. Ellison does not use the Chaplin reference to elevate the African American folklore Wheatstraw employs; he signifies on Chaplin's tramp by reinventing the tramp's ability to be an "agent of anarchy." When Wheatstraw riffs about Jack the Bear grabbing hold of his Chaplin pants, he uses the line, "Fe Fi Fo Fum," summoning the presence of another Jack, the boy with the beanstalk, from a European tradition, and yet another tramp who uses his cunning to get ahead. Peter Wheatstraw, Charlie Chaplin, and Jack are all mixed into the verbal soup.

The mixture shows up again in the scene where the narrator buys a yam from a street vendor. Although this may seem like a harmless thing to do, to the narrator it is an act of rebellion against the forces of modernism. As he smells the odor of the baked yams coming from the old wagon, he again feels the "surge of homesickness," remembering how his family used to bake the yams in the fireplace and carry them to school. Not only does he buy one to eat, he dares to eat it right there on the street: "I was eating while walking along the street. It was exhilarating. I no longer had to worry about who saw me or about what was proper" (264). He imagines his former schoolmates at the university seeing him and runs back to buy another. The street vendor is delighted and says, "I can see you one of these old-fashioned yam eaters" (266). The narrator agrees, responding, "They're my birthmark. I yam what I am!" (266). The narrator's play on words here is, of course, clever; he is claiming his childhood rural identity by eating the yams, and it is a moment in the text that supports the African American rural culture, but the words have another echo as well. As Mark Busby points out, "I yam what I yam," was the signature phrase of the 1930s cartoon character, Popeye the Sailor Man (83). Charlie Largent explains that the cartoon's creator, E. G. Segar, "must have bent over backward to create the most homely human ever

drawn. With one squinty eye, a pendulous nose and a sagging jaw that re-
sembled a baby's backside, Popeye was literally butt-ugly" (53). Popeye does
not try to be anything else, as his phrase indicates. *Invisible Man*'s narrator decides in this scene to celebrate his rural identity, which to him is not modern
and polished; it is comforting but ugly. The irony is that his announcement
of the embracing of a distinctly black identity (as opposed to the raceless
identity the Brotherhood will offer him) is voiced in an echo of a white cartoon character. The narrator then proceeds down the street to the scene of
the eviction and somehow gets himself involved in the middle of a fight between the police and a group of rioters. He may have eaten yams instead of
spinach, but the yams work to connect him to the old couple being evicted.

Just as Ellison spikes his humor with Western literature and popular culture from the 1930s, Welty's work displays some of these same influences.
Welty shares with Ellison the use of Harris's image of Brer Rabbit. Curly protests when Jack arranges for his truck to be towed to town by Judge Moody's
now-rescued Buick because Curly thinks it will make him look bad in front
of his customers and the voters. Lexie Renfro throws at Curly the insult that
"there's always *something* to come along to shorten the tail of the rabbit"
(397). The allusion is to Harris's story "How Mr. Rabbit Lost His Fine Bushy
Tail." Uncle Remus explains to the boy that rabbits used to have long tails,
but Brer Fox tricked Brer Rabbit into using his tail for bait when fishing. Instead of catching fish, Brer Rabbit discovers that his tail has been eaten off.
Although throughout most of the tales, Brer Rabbit is able to trick the other
characters, he is occasionally tricked himself. The same is true for the character of Curly, making Lexie's comment quite apt. Curly generally gets the
better of Jack. The trial, for example, over Jack stealing Curly's safe ends in
Jack going to prison. While Jack was gone, Curly managed to acquire Jack's
beloved truck. Being humbled by the condition of that same truck turns
Curly into the victim when he would rather play the trickster. The reference
to Brer Rabbit shows that one source for Curly's character and the humorous
scenes involving his rivalry with Jack is the mixed oral tradition involving the
trickster figure courtesy of Joel Chandler Harris/Uncle Remus.

However, just as Ralph Ellison incorporates contemporary popular culture into his humor, Welty's humor shows the influence of slapstick, particularly the 1930s comedy team The Three Stooges, which has a character
named Curly. The humor of The Three Stooges is predominantly physical
humor; the three characters hit each other, play tricks on each other, and generally vie for being the stupidest of the three. Jack and Curly's fights, which
often involve Jack's friend Aycock as well, echo both the physical comedy of
The Three Stooges as well as their extreme farce. When Curly, for example,

put the Beecham-Renfro family's gold ring in his safe, Jack retaliated by tying him up in a coffin that just happened to be in his store. Curly's favorite trick is to cut off Jack's and Aycock's shirttails and hang them in his store. The family's stories of these events always, of course, position Jack in the role of the hero and Curly as the villain, but the humor in their encounters owes a partial debt to contemporary culture.

In addition to using sources from the popular culture of 1930s, both Ellison and Welty inherit the mixed tradition of the frame tale I examined in chapter 1 and its close cousin, the tall tale. In *Invisible Man* we can see these traditions in the Trueblood episode, though it is perhaps the most surprising place to find an intersection of cultural traditions. Jim Trueblood is, after all, a *true* blood, an African American not co-opted by white society, in contrast to Dr. Bledsoe. Trueblood is the ultimate rural character, still living in a sharecropper cabin that was once slave quarters and making his living by being a master storyteller. A. Timothy Spaulding argues that Trueblood is both a "trickster figure" and a blues singer, thereby shaped from African American culture (489). If, however, we pay attention to the context of Trueblood's storytelling, we can see that Ellison borrows the scenario of a storyteller fooling an innocent audience from the frame tales written by Twain, Harris, and Chesnutt. Gillian Johns argues for the "presence of tall humor" in Trueblood's performance; she explains that even if "the tall tale has historically been a favorite genre for white men, we can approach Trueblood as someone who might know how to 'signify' in a tall tale because a parallel to white male tall humor exists in African American oral culture" (247).

Most critics have not seen Trueblood's story of impregnating his wife and daughter as part of the humor of the novel, and admittedly there is nothing funny about slave cabins, incest, and the deep-rooted racism evident in the scene, but if we see Trueblood's story as not a sociological picture of the South but as a performance in the African tradition of "lying" and in the analogous white tall tale tradition of telling a story to fool an audience, the humor becomes apparent.[9] As Trueblood begins the story, the narrator describes his tone as "taking on a deep, incantatory quality, as though he had told the story many, many times" (*Invisible Man* 54). Trueblood has in fact told the story many times, to the "boss man," the sheriff, and many other white men who seem to revel in its salacious details. Trueblood plays into the white men's prurient interest by crafting a story with heightened sexual content. He begins his story by telling about a seemingly irrelevant memory of a woman he used to live with in Mobile. The story rests on similes full of sexual innuendos. For example, he talks about seeing a watermelon, "split wide open a-layin' all spread out and cool and sweet on top of all the striped green ones like it's waitin' just for you so you can see how red and ripe and juicy it is and all the shiny black seeds it's got and all" (55–56). Trueblood ties this image to a "gal in a red dress and a wide straw hat goin' past you down a lane with the trees on both sides, and she's plump and juicy and kinda switchin' her tail 'cause she know you watchin'" (56). The girl becomes the piece of fruit ready to be consumed by the observer. Trueblood then diverts back to the story of how he mistakenly happened to have sex with his daughter but only follows this narrative line briefly before interrupting the plot with the description of a dream.

Trueblood uses his storytelling skills and sexual imagery to lure Mr. Norton in; the narrator says that Mr. Norton is "listening to Trueblood so intensely he didn't see me" (57). Now Trueblood is able to tell the most subversive story of all. He is able to tell a white man to his face a fantasy of walking in the front door of the master's house and being seduced by his white wife. He dreams that he enters Mr. Broadnax's house and gets trapped in a "big white bedroom" and although he "tries to git out," instead of finding a door, he sees a white lady stepping out of a clock only wearing a nightgown (57). She grabs him around the neck, and the only thing he can do is "[throw] her on the bed" (58). The narrator registers the shocking nature of the story, "How can he tell this to white men, I thought, when he knows they'll say that all Negroes do such things?" but Mr. Norton remains transfixed.

Trueblood seems to signal to the narrator that he is having fun at his white guest's expense: "Trueblood seemed to smile at me behind his eyes as he looked from the white man to me and continued," thereby establishing the inside audience (61). Many critics of this scene, including Houston A. Baker Jr., assume Trueblood is telling the truth.[10] Gillian Johns, however, argues that Trueblood's smile is the equivalent of a "rhetorical wink" that "[signals] the presence of tall humor" (245). Trueblood is using humor as a weapon to gain power. The white community has already responded to his story by giving him donations, and Mr. Norton hands him a hundred dollars before he leaves. Trueblood, however, gains something more important than money; he gains power through the performance. He knocks the powerful Mr. Norton out cold. Although he is as far away from Mr. Norton in his fancy custom shoes as Wheatstraw is from the men who literally make the plans, their laughter is at least an attempt to fight back. By exaggerating his tale enough to lure his innocent audience in, Trueblood tells a story worthy of the storytelling artist Mark Twain describes in "How to Tell a Story."

The Beecham-Renfro family has tall humor as part of their arsenal of weapons as well. Welty borrowed the tall humor at least in part from the southwestern humorists. Elizabeth Evans notes that "on October 29, 1946,

Lambert Davis (then an editor at Harcourt Brace) answered Miss Welty's request for copies of two classics of American humor—Judge Augustus Baldwin Longstreet's *Georgia Scenes* (1835) and Joseph Glover Baldwin's *The Flush Times of Alabama and Mississippi* (1853)" (21). The family's stories of its rivalry with Julia Mortimer certainly reflect the presence of tall humor. The town carpenter, Willy Trimble, stops by the reunion to announce the news of Julia's death, "Down fell she. End of *her*" (*Losing Battles* 230). When the new family member, Aunt Cleo, wonders why any of them would want to go to the wake of "somebody you don't know," a chorus of voices cries, "Know her? Suffered under her" (234). They claim the former schoolteacher was a "bane" and "our cross to bear" and furthermore "put an end to good fishing" (235, 240, 235). The stories they tell of this teacher create almost a caricature of a larger-than-life person. She lengthened the school year, carried milk to school to nourish underfed children, and switched students who did not keep up with their lessons. A group of her students won a spelling match against the Mississippi legislature, and even Beulah acknowledges, "She's responsible for a good deal I know right here today" (234). The family dislikes Julia because she wanted them to change, to "quit worshipping ourselves quite so wholehearted!" (236). She was the figure of progress and therefore a threat, even after her death. So the family members respond with humor; they tell tall tales to turn the strong schoolteacher into something comical. They tell, for example, the story of a cyclone that went straight through their town and was so strong that it picked up the Methodist church and put it down right beside the Baptist church. Despite the wind "shrieking" around the schoolhouse, Aunt Birdie claims, "I thought I saw [Julia Mortimer] throw herself down on the dictionary once, when it tried to get away" (237). Her love of books is a particular source of amusement for the family. Beulah claims, "The woman read more books than you could shake a stick at. I don't know what she thought was going to get her if she didn't" (240). When Gloria explains that Julia "liked to say, 'If it's going to be a case of Saint George and the Dragon, I might as well battle it left, right, front, back, center and sideways,'" Beulah retorts, "I'm glad Banner School didn't hear about that. Or me either, while I was one of her scholars. I'd had to run from a dragon, though that's about the only thing" (245). Gloria tries to explain that Julia Mortimer was Saint George and the dragon was Ignorance, but the family has succeeded in taming Julia by turning her into simply a character in their stories.

That both Ellison's African American folk character Trueblood and Welty's rural characters use tall humor as a weapon to render the modern characters ridiculous may point to some confluence in the oral traditions. Winifred Morgan examines African American oral tradition and the southwestern humorists and finds parallels specifically in the depiction of trickster characters who tell the con stories to fool their audiences. Morgan explains, "Although many students of literature have noted ways in which discrete works of African-American and other traditions have 'spoken' to one another, little has been written specifically about the influence of the humor of the Old Southwest, the states now generally referred to as the 'Deep South.' In fact, spelling out how each tradition has spoken to the other is a challenge, even though the 'heroes' of both traditions are tricksters" (210). One area where he does find influence is the depiction of forbidden subjects. According to Morgan, the southwest tricksters "assaulted" the period's "good taste" and opened up the realm of possibility in terms of spurious content (212). This association of African American tricksters with southwestern humor may in part explain how Trueblood gets away with telling the incredible story that he tells. Mr. Norton as well as the other white men who listen to his story think they are hearing a true story of forbidden sexuality in Trueblood's story of incest with his daughter, a story that is particularly titillating to Mr. Norton because of his strange obsession with his own daughter. But the explanation Trueblood offers for how he ended up in that precarious position is in the form of a dream, a pure fiction, and is loaded with an even greater sexual taboo than incest in its depiction of miscegenation, as *Absalom, Absalom!* demonstrates. The white woman lures him into the bedroom. If Morgan is correct that African American tricksters inherit the ability from the southwestern humorists to poke fun at the forbidden, Trueblood receives a huge inheritance indeed.

Because Ellison's debt to white Western culture is evident in the parts of the novel normally labeled African American folklore, his novel proves his declaration that "the heel bone is, after all, connected, through its various linkages, to the head bone" (*Collected Essays* 253). But Ellison argues that the reverse is true as well; an idea of white American culture cannot be fashioned without considering the influence of African American culture: "The master artisans of the South were slaves, and white Americans have been walking Negro walks, talking Negro flavored talk, . . . dancing Negro dances and singing Negro melodies" (256). The African American tradition of signifying appears both in Trueblood's dream and in Welty's depiction of the trial scene in *Losing Battles*. Henry Louis Gates Jr. defines signifying as "repetition with a signal difference" (51). Trueblood's dream signifies on Edgar Allan Poe's "The Masque of the Red Death." Ellison does not just allude to Western sources and stories but changes them, by providing that signal difference that allows him to speak back to the canon. The narrator of *Invisible Man* assures the reader in the second sentence of the novel that he is "not a spook like those who haunted Edgar Allan Poe," but one of Poe's spooks finds her way into the trickster's tale (3). In Trueblood's dream, he goes to the house of Mr. Broadnax looking for "some fat meat" (57). He breaks taboo by entering the house through the front door and then by entering another room. He finds himself in a "big white bedroom," where "everything in the room was white." In Poe's gothic tale, the wealthy Prospero tries to isolate himself from the "red death," which is killing all his countrymen, by secluding himself with his friends in his estate. He throws a giant party in a set of seven rooms, each decorated in a particular color. The ominous tone of the story comes from a grandfather clock in the last room, which is colored black; the clock chimes the hour every hour until midnight, when a masked man, dressed up as the red death appears among the guests thereby killing everyone. Ellison plays with the motifs from Poe's story. He includes the strange clock but makes the frightening room all white, instead of black. Instead of a spook in the form of a masked figure, the scary monster in this gothic tale is a white woman wearing a white nightgown who traps Trueblood. Ellison inserts a bit of the gothic tradition from Poe into his rural African American storyteller's tale, but he also rewrites it so that the gothic element comes from sexual taboos about white women. He turns Poe's symbolic language on its head, so whiteness becomes the mark of terror.[11] This signal difference speaks back to the way Poe and other gothic writers use blackness, both as color and as a racial marker. The dark humor of Trueblood's dream works on two levels. Trueblood uses the dream to laugh at the supposedly superior white man, while Ellison uses the allusions to play with his literary ancestors. Signifying proves to be a useful weapon in *Invisible Man.*

Welty also uses signifying in *Losing Battles* proving Ellison's point about white America "talking Negro flavored talk" even when they are not conscious of it. There is no way of knowing how aware Welty was of this element of African American folklore, but Kenneth Bearden has argued that signifying occurs also in Welty's story "Powerhouse," which depicts the blues player Fats Waller. Henry Louis Gates Jr. explains in his discussion of signifying that the image associated with the trickster figure in African American oral tradition is often the monkey. Bearden argues that Welty includes the signifying monkey in "Powerhouse": "What is even more intriguing and startling, perhaps, is how Welty incorporates a traditional African American folktale figure into the story, a figure that not too many of her contemporary white readers would know; Powerhouse is referred to once as a 'monkey.'" Together with his behavior, his appearance causes Bearden to suggest, "We cannot help but make the connection between Powerhouse and the Signifying Monkey, that trickster figure who is capable of causing calamity (especially to the Lion) through his mastery of language" (71). In *Losing Battles* Welty plays with signifying in Jack's trial. When Judge Moody asked Jack why he stole Curly's safe and tied him up in a coffin, Jack answered, "Well, it's because he's aggravating" (54). The judge then asked Jack to define aggravating and give him an example. Jack dodged the question, responding, "He'd just have to show you himself" (54). In telling this story at the reunion, the family ponders whether Jack just could not tell a good story or whether he was protecting his sister, whose flirtation with Curly started the fight. The judge tried to understand Jack's motivation: "The storekeeper aggravated you, so you carried off his safe. Was it your idea to rob him?" Jack responded, "No sir, just to aggravate him" (55). Judge Moody seemed to get nowhere questioning Jack because instead of telling the facts, he referred to Curly's character, "He's aggravating" and instead of a motive, he claimed he wanted to in turn "aggravate" Curly. The end of the trial and the punch line of the family's story of it is the judge's decision that Jack was guilty of "aggravated battery," turning the "aggravated" from its normal function of modifying the action, battery, to modifying the person, Jack, who was aggravated and thus committed battery. In the retelling of the story, Beulah says that the judge "made a monkey" out of Jack. The family made a clown, an image from Western tradition, out of the judge while enacting their Christian-inspired ceremony of forgiving him, but when the text plays with the African American tradition of signifying the image is that of the signifying monkey. The family's forgiving ceremony may then be their attempt to restage or signify on the trial as they get to be the tricksters and judge the judge. They then repeat their "forgiving" of the judge until it too bears that signal difference. Bearden's explanation of Welty's knowledge is intriguing and fits Welty's use of folklore in *Losing Battles* as well; he claims that "it is highly probable that Welty ran across this African American trickster legend while working with the WPA" (71). If so, Welty employs it well. She incorporates the technique from African American culture to show how the judge and Jack with their different definitions of "aggravating" are from different worlds. The family uses signifying as another means to laugh at their opponents.

***

After staging the battles between the forces of folk culture and modernism, both authors decide to leave the battles without a clear victor. The two novels instead end in ambivalence, which causes some critics to complain about the whimper when they wanted the bang. Marcus Klein argues that *Invisible Man* "doesn't finally go anywhere," which then "led Ellison to the desperate, empty, unreasonable, and programmatic optimism of the last few pages of the novel" (*After Alienation* 109). Houston A. Baker Jr.'s complaints are even more biting; he suggests that Ellison should have predicted and valued the grassroots movement that would lead to the civil rights movement: "No, it is not that Ellison missed the futuristic black 'underground' altogether. He simply failed, or refused, to inscribe the process of that 'underground' transforming itself into a field of revolutionary energy that changed the ways of black American folk for all time" ("Failed" 6). In a review in 1970 of Welty's novel, Joyce Carol Oates not only argues that "the concerns of *Losing Battles* are extinct" but that Welty "has no 'ideas' whatsoever. She has no political or spiritual arguments. She has no social arguments. She is aware of, but does not insist upon, the injustices of the economic establishment" (120). The ambivalence that the critics complain about might be, however, also part of Welty's and Ellison's experiments with oral storytelling. The same oral storytelling that comes from and marks the confluence of cultures also leads to a searching and valuing of the middle ground. In oral culture tellers and listeners search for a verbal space for interaction. Instead of victory, the value is on connection. Welty and Ellison were both modern outsiders to the "folk" they met through their WPA experiences, and they both value the intersection of the modern and the folk. Welty looks for a connection between rural folk culture and the modern world outside Banner; the connections she makes are between classes. Ellison's middle ground is more dangerous because it is the mixing of races, the miscegenation of teller and audience.

Some critics of *Losing Battles* have confronted the ambivalence of the novel by supplying their own interpretations of who wins the battle. Franziska Gygax, for example, argues that Welty parodies the family but not Gloria or Julia. In her reading Jack is replaced by these two female characters in the role of hero: "Jack does not meet the expectations of a hero if we compare him to Julia and Gloria, the two female protagonists. They critically question their social and cultural environments, whereas Jack never does" (91). Jan Gretlund counters with a reading that places Welty's work in a "cultural continuity of Agrarian ideas from their origin in the rural South to their importance in today's South," which leads him to a conclusion: "I am convinced that Welty in this novel chooses between the farmers and the proponents of progress, and that the writer's stand is finally with and unmistakably for the farmers and their ancient values" (271). The irony is, of course, if critics can make good arguments with persuasive evidence for both sides, then there is some ambivalence in the presentation of the sides. Other critics take up this argument, claiming that neither side can claim victory. Shelia Stroup, for example, argues that "Miss Welty does not take sides in *Losing Battles*. Instead she shows us the strengths and weaknesses of both sides in their 'eternal tug-of-war' and makes us see that one kind of mind, one kind of world, must be tempered by the other, that there needs to be a reconciliation, a bridge between the widely divergent points of view" (47).[12]

This reconciliation occurs because of the storytelling. After Welty crafts a plot that wrecks the judge's car and forces the modern world to meet the rural folk during the reunion, the two sides have to listen to each other's stories. After the family members forgive Judge Moody and turn Julia Mortimer into a caricature through their humorous stories, they have to take their turn as the listeners when Judge Moody starts to talk. When Willy Trimble shows the reunion a speller he found under Julia's pillow with "M-Y-W-I-L-L" scratched on it, the judge finally speaks up and takes charge. The family is surprised that he, too, knew Julia; Beulah asks, "Are you about to tell us you come into this story too?" (290). His story of Julia is very different from the family's version. Julia acted as a mentor to him, encouraged his studies, and persuaded him to remain in Mississippi. When his wife wonders if he ever courted Julia, he responds, "Why, every young blade in Ludlow was wild about Miss Julia Mortimer at one time" (304). Although he did not court her, he lists others who did, using the word "aspire," much to the shock of his audience. In contrast to the family who laughed at Julia's inability to get the rural folk to change their ways, the judge mourns what happened to her, saying, "It could make a stone cry" (306). Not only does the family have to listen to the judge's stories, he reads Julia's will and letter to them, so that even Julia Mortimer gets to speak to the reunion from the grave. Aunt Birdie protests, "Looks like it's our fate to sit through one more lesson," and wonders, "Ain't we remembered enough about Miss Julia Mortimer?" (297). Judge Moody's response demonstrates why one side is not enough: "Your memory's got a dozen holes in it. And some sad mistakes" (297). In her will Julia's devotion to the school is evident in her wish to be buried under its steps, and she "constitutes" everyone in Banner as her mourners. In the letter she expresses the understanding she gained in hindsight about why she could not win over all her students when their "survival instinct" meant that they had to fight her.

This exchange of stories has an effect in the discussion over whether Jack and Gloria's marriage is legitimate. The family's stories have positioned Jack and Gloria as first cousins. Gloria was an orphan and had assumed that her mother lived far away from Banner. Granny Vaughn tells the story of a red-haired girl named Rachel, who looked much like Gloria, staying at their home one year and then shows an old postcard from the family's own Sam

Dale Beecham to Rachel signed "your husband." When Beulah realizes that the blood ties might make her son's marriage void and her grandchild illegitimate, she tells the story of neglecting one day to watch Sam Dale as a baby. When his clothes caught on fire, Beulah admits, her carelessness caused an injury that would have prevented him from fathering children. The judge, of course, views their stories as simply "Hearsay, Hearsay" claiming that "they've told a patched-together family story and succeeded in bringing out no more evidence than if their declared intention had been to conceal it" (322). He has to admit, however, that his "kind of evidence," that is, written proof, is also missing; if there had been any birth records, they would have been destroyed in the courthouse fire. In the face of this dilemma, Judge Moody makes an uncharacteristic decision. He decides he has to "[take] the law into my own hands" to help Jack. With the baby Lady May in their midst, the judge decides, "I think we'll have to close one eye over that everlasting baby" (325). His decision is also a nod to Julia; he exclaims with a sigh, "I suppose, if I was the first of Miss Julia's protégés, [Gloria] was her last" (325). Neither side actually wins since it is never revealed if Jack and Gloria are cousins; they just all decide to let it be.

From this point forward the novel abounds with images of compromise. The characters end up rescuing the judge's Buick by making a chain of the Buick, Curly's truck, the school bus, and two mules. They edge their way down the mountain, stopping to pick up schoolchildren along the way. When Jack and the judge part by shaking hands, the judge shows what he has learned about Jack's world by saying, "I hope you save the hay" (421). Although Jack and Curly start their slapstick routine again, Jack's sister announces her intention to marry Curly. Jack cries, "Our battles'll be called off before they start! We'll all be one happy family!" (412). Instead of a violent bang, Welty's comedy ends how comedies are supposed to, with the announcement of a wedding. The storytelling leads to a middle ground.

Ellison's search for the middle ground goes in a different direction. His narrator is faced with the extremes of believing in a world wholly segregated by race or wholly uninformed by race. Although he bounces back and forth between these two poles, in the end the text suggests yet a third option, racial mixing. *Invisible Man* contains many metaphors of racial mixing, but the most obvious is the white paint at the paint factory. When the narrator shows up to work at the factory, his first job is to put black liquid into the white paint. Although he questions his boss about the wisdom of mixing the two, he is told that this is the secret to the company's best "Optic White" paint. His boss, Mr. Kimbro, claims, "It's the purest white that can be found. Nobody makes a paint any whiter" (202). The narrator sees a gray tinge in the painted samples, but Kimbro only sees the brilliant white. The irony is clear; there is no pure white, and the colors and races are already mixed. In fact, the narrator himself is the product of mixed blood, as revealed during the fight at the beginning of the novel when one of the other boys calls him "ginger-colored" (21). In his epilogue he claims that America is likewise a mixture: "Our fate is become one, and yet many—This is not prophecy, but description. Thus one of the greatest jokes in the world is the spectacle of the whites busy escaping blackness and becoming blacker every day, and the blacks striving toward whiteness, becoming dull and gray" (577).

Storytelling is again the key to finding this middle ground, although here it is not so much the storytelling *in* the novel but the storytelling *of* the novel. The storytelling in the novel most often works to establish racial barriers, as when Trueblood smiles at the narrator but fools Mr. Norton or when Wheatstraw stops to speak to the narrator because he is "from down home" (173). The storytelling of the novel is the entire narrative between the prologue and the epilogue, which is told as a flashback by the narrator to an audience. Michel Fabre writes about this audience, the "narratee," to explain how Ellison's narrator tries to create a relationship with the implied reader. Fabre points out that the prologue and epilogue both use present tense so that "the protagonist speaks to, i.e., addresses actively, a narratee whom he wants to involve in his (fictionalized) performance. The form is lively, quick, apparently spontaneous" (537). I would add that the form is oral; in the prologue and epilogue Ellison tries to replicate the dynamics of oral storytelling by making the narrator the storyteller and the reader the audience. The "lively" action of the telling helps the reader feel as if he or she is participating. Fabre points out that the narrator assumes responses or interjections on the part of the narratee. From the very beginning lines, when the narrator says, "I am an invisible man. No, I am not a spook like those who haunted Edgar Allan Poe; nor am I one of your Hollywood-movie ectoplasms," he speaks as if the reader/listener is interrupting. He also uses second person repeatedly to involve this narratee in the action as when, for example, he assures his audience, "I say all this to assure you that it is incorrect to assume that, because I'm invisible and live in a hole, I am dead" (6). Twice, as Fabre points out, the narrator claims he can hear his audience speak back to him. In the prologue, he says, "I can hear you say, 'What a horrible, irresponsible bastard!' And you're right. I leap to agree with you" (14). This is echoed in the epilogue when he says, "'Ah,' I can hear you say, 'so it was all a build-up to bore us with his buggy jiving'" (581). Not only is the reader posed as a listener, the reader is given a speaking role in the storytelling.

Fabre's most interesting argument about this narratee, however, is that he is cast as white. In the prologue, after complaining that the blond man could not see him because whites cannot see blacks, thereby making them invisible, the narrator says to his audience, "Since you never recognize me even when in closest contact with me, and since, no doubt, you'll hardly believe that I exist, it won't matter if you know that I tapped a power line leading into the building and ran it into my hole in the ground" (13). To Fabre, this means that Ellison is trying to appeal to the Everyman and make his novel a "universal parable" (541). This may be true, but in a reading that pays attention to the mixture of cultures, the novel becomes not universal as much as mixed. When the narrator concludes the book with the question "Who knows but that, on the lower frequencies, I speak for you?" Ellison finds within oral storytelling a middle ground, a verbal space for the narrator and audience to meet (581).[13] The narrator tells the reader to call him "Jack-the-Bear"; he plays the part of the trickster telling a story about his own life but in the end claiming it is a story about every life. What critics find in *Invisible Man* as ambivalence or a lack of action may be instead a concerted effort to reach an audience. Winther claims that the "socially responsible role" the narrator chooses is that of the literary artist (282). The telling of his story is his action. We can see how truly radical this action is once we realize that he is telling his tale to a white audience. Ellison takes the frame tales Harris and Chesnutt use further by imagining a white audience who will actually be on the same frequency.

***

Although Eudora Welty and Ralph Ellison knew and apparently admired each other, there are no direct connections between their works. Both, however, draw from the same arsenal of mixed cultural heritage including tall tales, signifying, and popular culture in the 1930s. The confluence between these two writers appears in the similar depictions of these tools as weapons the folk can use against the forces of modernism. The family in *Losing Battles*, eking out a living in rural Mississippi, and the characters in *Invisible Man*, trying to survive a segregated urban existence in New York City, should have nothing in common, but the shared inheritance of southern oral tradition causes them both to use humor to fight back. Welty's and Ellison's experiences with the WPA cause them to write sympathetically of the folks' attempts to preserve their cultures through their use of stories.

The storytellers in these works have a common cause as well: the threat to their identity from the forces of modernism. In the modern world, writing is king, and the battle between the forces of modernism and folk culture is in part a battle over words. In John Steinbeck's *Grapes of Wrath*, one character complains, "Ever' time Pa seen writin', somebody took somepin away from 'im" (73–74). The family in *Losing Battles* seems defenseless against the clearly superior intellect of Judge Moody just as the elderly couple evicted in *Invisible Man* cannot fight the system putting them out on the street. But the folk use their oral abilities to poke fun at the threats to their identity. Laughter does not seem as potent a force as money or violence, but the ability to laugh shows resilience. Welty said of her own book: "I feel it's more a novel of admiration for the human being who can cope with any condition, even ignorance, and keep a courage, a joy of life, even, that's unquenchable" ("Interior World" 52). The narrator of *Invisible Man* learns to laugh as well. In his epilogue he tells of running into Mr. Norton in New York; Norton is lost in the subway and asks for directions. The narrator reminds Mr. Norton that he is his "destiny," but Mr. Norton has no memory of him, Trueblood, or the Golden Day. The narrator explains that he "stood there laughing hysterically. I laughed all the way back to my hole" (579). The narrator has learned the lesson of Trueblood and Wheatstraw; in the face of overwhelming odds, you just have to laugh.

4
Haunted by Stories

Ernest Gaines's *A Gathering of Old Men*
and Ellen Douglas's *Can't Quit You, Baby*

When Quentin Compson complains in *Absalom, Absalom!* about the ghosts haunting him, "listening, having to listen, to one of the ghosts which had refused to lie still even longer than most had, telling him about old ghost-times," he is not alone (5). Being pestered by ghosts is indeed common in southern fiction, but even as the characters and writers of contemporary southern literature continue to ward off the phantoms of the past, the ghosts they see and the stories they tell have changed. In discussing the haunting present in *Turning South Again*, Houston A. Baker Jr. starts with his child-hood fears of the "Blue Man," a monstrous image the children created to explain the tyranny of white people. He then moves to his adult sense of be-ing haunted by his late father and by Booker T. Washington, both idealists who embraced the modernist idea of high (that is, Western, white) culture as the key to advancement. Baker explains that the South as "home" always holds both aversion and attraction, causing him to engage in a "deeply am-bivalent rehashing of the past" (18). This rehashing of the past is the very basis of haunting, the intrusion of the past into the present. The change in contemporary fiction comes from which past is intruding. For Faulkner's characters it is the past in which they lost the war, in which the American dream Sutpen chases is elusive, and in which the Eden of southern land-scape is tainted by the greed of men. The past Baker rehashes is quite differ-ent because the focus has changed: "I often stay awake at night. Ghostly em-anations of southern economies of violence against the black body toss and turn me. I have nightmares populated by posh-suited apologists for millions of African bodies displaced and disappeared by a Euro-American consumer revolution and transatlantic trade" (9). The ghosts of the African bodies that Baker describes are those haunting the two contemporary works I will examine, Ernest Gaines's *A Gathering of Old Men* and Ellen Douglas's *Can't Quit You, Baby*. In these works the past intrudes into the present in the form of stories previously untold and ghosts of black bodies previously "displaced and disappeared."

Written in the 1980s, the novels reflect a contemporary interest in exploring opportunities for racial crossing, although both are set in the heart of the civil rights era: *Can't Quit You, Baby* in the 1960s and *A Gathering of Old Men* in the 1970s. Both authors explore racial crossing by having their African American characters tell stories to white audiences, linking their texts back to the oral storytelling depicted by Joel Chandler Harris and Charles Chesnutt. The difference here is that the storytelling works to effect cross-racial understanding, although not without some difficulty. White listeners must overcome apathy and aversion to the stories of the black characters. In fact Gaines and Douglas depict the white characters' struggles to understand as the lack of a basic sense—either sight or hearing. With some evident progress, both novels have fairly positive endings. Previously untold or repressed stories are heard, and the black ghosts haunting the southern present get their day.

Both writers inherit the attention to oral storytelling and the strategies for making the written seem oral from the previous writers in this study. Ellen Douglas speaks of her "delight of discovery" on first reading Eudora Welty but claims William Faulkner as the greater influence: "When I was in my middle teens, I thought Faulkner was God—and then after I began to write, I began to try to get away from it because it was so pervasive and so crippling."[1] When asked in an interview how he made the leap from oral storytelling to written literature, Gaines acknowledged the influence of Joyce, Twain, and Faulkner, explaining, "Twain and Faulkner are the fathers of this, this combination of that oral tradition and then integrating it into a literary tradition. So it's something that I have inherited from having that kind of background and then having studied literature" (*Porch* 8). The background he mentions is the plantation, where storytelling was popular. Gaines even shares with modern writers a debt to the WPA; while working on *The Autobiography of Miss Jane Pittman*, Gaines explains, his "Bible was *Lay My Burden Down*, a collection of short WPA interviews with ex-slaves recorded during the 30's. I used that book to get the rhythm of speech and an idea of how the ex-slaves would talk about themselves" (*Conversations* 94). Gaines also credits Faulkner with influencing his craft of writing dialect: "He has made me listen to dialects over again. I find that so many of my contemporary black writers probably don't listen well to dialects around them. . . . So reading Faulkner just makes me pay more attention to dialect, to dialogue" (*Conver-*

sations 66). Although Gaines expresses admiration for several African American writers, particularly Jean Toomer, he admits that "no black writer had influence on me" because he lacked access early on to their works (*Porch* 33). The cultural inheritance Gaines and Douglas get from writers such as Twain and Faulkner is, however, a racially mixed one.

Douglas and Gaines take this inheritance and push the experimentation with form, evident in the works of the modernist writers Hurston, Faulkner, Ellison, and Welty, further by extending the disruptions caused by the intrusion of oral storytelling into a written narrative. In Gaines's novel the experimentation becomes a study in point of view with various characters taking turns telling and retelling the stories, showing the layers of constructions. Douglas experiments with the locus of the narrator as well but instead of splitting the point of view, she uses metafictional comments by the narrator to lead the reader to question the choice and positioning of the stories. By highlighting the constructed nature of the stories, these postmodern texts point to the constructed nature of all narratives. In this open space, repressed stories are able to resurface, and the ghosts from the past have a chance to enter the meaning-making process because the truth is still in flux. Gaines and Douglas play with the dynamics of oral storytelling by including the reader in the search for meaning as well. The reader must sift through the various constructions in Douglas's novel and must act as the "live" audience for the retelling of the stories in Gaines's novel. This inclusion of the reader, however, means that, along with the fictional characters, Houston A. Baker Jr., and the ever-complaining Quentin, the reader too must become haunted by the past.

In using oral storytelling Gaines and Douglas are, to borrow Baker's words, turning south again, but their turn south is not a return in the sense of covering old ground. Like the southern writers before them, they find in oral storytelling a tool they can revise to fit the concerns of their time period. In using oral storytelling to explore racial crossing, they are engaged in questions that reflect their contemporary context: What is the role of race in the contemporary post–civil rights world? How does the past history of the South affect the present? What do you do with the ghosts?

***

The catalysts for the storytelling in both novels are characters feeling haunted by a past that refuses to be silent and by ghosts whose stories need to be told. In *A Gathering of Old Men* the old men appear near ghost-like themselves as they gather at Mathu's house. Mathu has supposedly killed Beau

Boutan, son of Fix, the infamously cruel Cajun. Chimley, who is seventy-two years old, explains the significance of this particular murder, "I had never knowed in all my life where a black man had killed a white man in this parish" (28). The black men, however, also do something they have never done before. Instead of hiding in fear of Fix and his friends, who are expected to "ride" and perform a "stringing," they gather at Mathu's house with guns, each claiming that he shot Beau in an act of defiance against the law and the unofficial rules of race in their world.

On the way to Mathu's house, they stop first at a graveyard. This first episode is told through the voice of Cherry, who says that the graveyard has a few markers but that the black families were basically mixed together. More importantly, the graveyard ties Cherry and his friends back to the distant but still vital past: "That old graveyard had been the burial ground for black folks ever since the time of slavery. I was seventy-four, and I had grandparents in there" (44). When Jacob begins to pull weeds from his sister Tessie's grave, Cherry tells the story of how she was killed by white men because she was "one of them great big pretty mulatto gals who messed around with the white man and the black man" (45). Jacob's family, mulattos who were "quality" people, refused to accept her body, and she was buried in the black cemetery. Cherry reflects on the importance of this past event to their present act: "Maybe that's why Jacob was here today, to make up for what he had done his sister over thirty years ago" (45). The other men then follow Jacob's example and clear off their family graves. When Dirty Red wonders if the graveyard will still be there when he dies because "these white folks coming up today don't have no respect for the dead," he indicates the importance of the past and its ghosts for African Americans. Anissa Wardi examines the cemetery scene in reference to the sacredness of the land and concludes that "the ancestors are the forgotten ghosts who, despite the changing topography and population shifts, remain in and of the Southern land" (39). This fictional cemetery has a simulacrum of sorts in Gaines's current life. Gaines and his wife have rescued the African American cemetery next to their house, where his ancestors and other slave families were buried for generations. Just as the characters in his novel do, Gaines attests to his connection to the past through these graves: "If I didn't have those people back there, I would never have had anything to write about. . . . That's where I got all my stories from. My life is from them" (Seelye). The old men in the novel eat pecans from the graveyard, establishing their dependence on the past by literally feeding on it.

From the graveyard, the men march to Mathu's house "like soldiers," though before their experience in the graveyard Chimley had described the group of elderly men as a sad bunch, not "ready for battle" (Gathering 43).

Braced with the force of the past, they are now ready to do battle and to tell the long repressed stories of these dead ancestors publicly. That the ghosts are the impetus for the storytelling is confirmed when Tucker tells the story of his brother Silas. Silas kept farming after the Cajuns had taken over most of the land and were using machines. After Silas raced his mules against a tractor and won, he was killed: "They won. But they wasn't supposed to win. How can flesh and blood and nigger win against white man and machine? So they beat him. They took stalks of cane and they beat him and beat him and beat him" (96). Tucker explains that his guilt comes from his refusal to help his brother: "And I didn't do nothing but stand there and watch them beat my brother down to the ground" (97). Tucker then walks away from Mathu's house, faces the graveyard, and yells, "Forgive me!" (97). Rufe, who is telling this part of the narrative, comments that "all of us had stood here—in one of these old yards—and we had all hollered toward that graveyard" (97). The past has haunted these old men, but this day they summon the courage to tell ghost stories.

In *Can't Quit You, Baby* the haunting past drives the storytelling as well. The novel focuses on two individuals, who are first introduced by the narrator as the reader would see them from the outside, "the white woman" and "the black woman." The white woman is Cornelia and the black woman is Julia or "Tweet," who works as Cornelia's housekeeper. When Tweet arrives for work in the morning, she often brings Cornelia gifts, such as wildflowers or a story. Although Tweet's stories cover various aspects of her life, the longest and most important story she tells Cornelia is about her grandfather and how Tweet was "born lucky" because she was raised by this man (18). The bad luck came when her father entered her life when she was fifteen and her grandfather subsequently died. In relating this crucial turning point to Cornelia, Tweet explicitly constructs the event as a ghost story.

She explains to Cornelia that her father, Julius, and his wife, Claree, arrived in November, shortly after Halloween, a holiday she quickly dismisses because of its "foolishness" when there is "too much real evil, too many real spirits to be afraid of" (26). Tweet then leans across the table to Cornelia and says, "The dead live. . . . The dead stay in the place where they die and their power is in that place" (26). While Cornelia tries to ignore this seemingly outlandish pronouncement, Tweet continues, "My grandpa's soul is in the furrow by the turnrow where he died. When I'm feeling strong enough to bear it, I can go down on the edge of the cypress break by the turnrow where he lay down, and he is with me" (26). When she claims that her grandfather speaks to her, Cornelia says, "No," because she is "embarrassed by this foolishness" (27). Tweet claims that her grandfather often even sings to her but concludes by stating that her point is "we—our people—don't have time for these play-like ghosts. These dress-up children that go around begging for candy" (27). Tweet is concerned about real spirits, specifically the ghost of her grandfather, who died because his son Julius wanted money so badly that he was willing to kill his family to get it.

What Julius did not realize when he set fire to the house that Tweet lives in with her grandfather is that the bulk of the money is not tied up in the farm but is hidden in a bee tree in the cypress brake behind the house. Tweet later tells the story to Cornelia of her cleverness in getting this money, but in explaining the presence of her grandfather's ghost in her life, she relates yet another ghost story tied to the first. She tells Cornelia that the lights often seen in the cypress brake are from the ghost of a man who buried his gold there during the Civil War, a white man who "made his fortune selling our people" (28). Her story reveals that he was eaten by the devil, in the shape of an alligator, and that his gold is still hidden in the brake. This embedded story ties the events of Tweet's life and her own oppression at the hands of white people clearly back to the past, just as the cemetery ties the old men back to the past of slavery. The ill-gotten gold from the enslavement of Africans and the hidden gold her father, with the help of white men, will try to take from her are connected in their hiding place in the haunted cypress brake. The ghost of her grandfather pushes Tweet to tell these stories to Cornelia and to make public the hidden, repressed, and ignored.

***

With the haunting as catalyst, the African American characters in both novels are compelled to tell stories as a means of gaining power in the present to make up for the oppressions of the past. Gaines and Douglas use the racially mixed oral tradition they inherit to give their characters the power of the teller of the tale. The teller is able to construct history or to create a fictional world. The teller can tell the truth that has been ignored or play God and create a world more to his or her liking. Language becomes the tool, and occasionally the weapon, of this force. At the very beginning of *Can't Quit You, Baby* the narrator highlights the connection of language to power when she introduces the two characters and describes their relationship. Cornelia does not like the word "servant" to describe Tweet, and "mistress" carries uncomfortable sexual connotations, so the narrator concludes, "Let's settle for housekeeper and employer." The very description of their relationship is charged with issues of power in the term "servant," and with the overtones of slavery in the consideration of "mistress." The narrator then explains that although everyone else calls Tweet by her nickname, Cornelia decides, "I think I'll call you Julia, if you don't mind" (6). She also refuses to call Tweet's husband by his nickname, "Nig," which is again too reminiscent of slavery, and so she settles on "Mr. Carrier" (6). The power to decide names, a key factor of identity, is held in the white woman's hands. Gaines's novel depicts language and power as similarly contained in the white world, and one signal of this connection is found again in the use of names. Gaines heads each chapter with the two names of the person narrating that section; the first is the legal, given name, such as "George Eliot, Jr.," and the second is the nickname, such as "Snookum." Joseph Griffin points out that the dual names expose power structures: "Whites address blacks by their nicknames, some of which are pejorative, but blacks do not address whites by nicknames" (91). An example is Chimley, whose nickname comes from his dark skin. Mat explains, "He didn't mind his friends calling him Chimley, 'cause he knowed we didn't mean nothing. But he sure didn't like them white folks calling him Chimley" (*Gathering* 40). Although Chimley tells white people his name is Robert Louis Stevenson Banks, "all they did was laugh at him, and they went on calling him Chimley anyhow" (40). The ability to determine one's own name is crucial to constructing an identity. The power clearly lies in the use of language, so to obtain power Tweet and Chimley will have to become storytellers.

The old men gathered at Mathu's house tell two kinds of stories in their bid to gain power. The first is a fictional story about how each came that morning to Mathu's house and shot Beau, and the second is a personal story from the past, often the story of someone buried in the cemetery. They start constructing their fictional stories when they arrive at Mathu's house, rehearsing for their later performance in front of Sheriff Mapes, when they will each claim to be guilty. Candy Marshall, a direct descendant of the Marshalls (who owned the plantation during slavery) and the current owner of the land most of the old men live on, actually begins the fictionalizing when she claims to have killed Beau in order to protect Mathu, who is a father figure to her. Candy is also the reason the men know about the murder and the originator of the plan for them to show up with shotguns, so that the police will not be able to arrest Mathu. Although the gathering is started by this white woman, the old men quickly take over the storytelling as they concoct reasons for being at the Marshall plantation that day with a gun in hand and for killing Beau. Mat, for example, who does not live nearby, claims he was out hunting for a chicken hawk that had been eating his chickens and had "followed him all the way from Medlow to Marshall" (53).

These fictional stories of violence, half-told in jest, eventually lead to true stories from the past as the men try to explain their motives for killing Beau. Yank, for example, tells of his career as a horsebreaker: "Lot of these rich white folks you see riding these fine horses in Mardi Gras parades, prancing all over the place, I broke them horses" (98). His career and his usefulness to the white people end because "they ain't got no more horses to break no more. The tractors, the cane cutters—and I ain't been nothing ever since" (99). He is now seen as "trifling" because he is out of work. He then connects this story of his past with his motive for killing Beau: "Maybe that's why I shot the man who took the horse from me" (99). Telling these stories has given Yank a sense of power. When the deputy tries to record the confession and starts spelling his name "Yank. Y-a-n–," Yank interrupts him to tell him his name is "Sylvester J. Battley. Be sure and spell Sylvester and Battley right, if you can" (99). Gable, who Rufe says has hardly been out of his house in twenty years, next tells the story of his son, "He wasn't but sixteen years old, half out of his mind, they put him in the 'lectric chair on the word of a poor white trash. They knowed what kind of gal she was. . . . But they put him in that chair 'cause she said he raped her" (101). Gable's story turns gruesome as he describes how the chair did not work properly, and it took the executioners several attempts to kill his son. Just as Yank did, Gable then connects this past story to the present: "And that's why I kilt Beau, Mr. Sheriff. He was just like that trashy white gal. He was just like them who throwed my boy in that 'lectric chair and pulled that switch. No, he wasn't born yet, but the same blood run in all their vein" (102).

In telling these stories of the past, the old men gain power by claiming the right to construct that history and to point out the wrongs done to them by white people. Herman Beavers argues that the storytelling "destabilizes the regulatory machinery that has shaped their sense of possibility and becomes the vehicle that carries the old men into transgressive space. The negations that have shaped their lives become sites of affirmation because they enter the realm of narration. And in each instance, the old men use narrative to give voice to the past" (167). Giving voice to the past is certainly a bid for power, but the stories gain even more force in their connection to the present. The connections Yank and Gable draw between their past experiences and their motives for killing Beau are certainly tenuous at best, but the links between the true past stories and the fictional present stories are crucial in their attempt to gain power. By setting up the stories as cause and effect, the old men claim to have the power needed to kill the oppressor, symbolized this day by Beau Boutan, and claim that the power originated as an answer to a past wrong. Telling the stories leads to the will if not the actual chance to strike back; power follows language.

Tweet gains power by telling stories that expose the oppression and racism she has faced. The first story she tells Cornelia, for example, is of Wayne Jones and exposes the vulnerability of black women to sexual harassment. Cornelia sparks this story by mentioning to Tweet that she had seen the obituary of Jones, Tweet's former employer, in the newspaper. Tweet's pleased reaction is certainly not what Cornelia was expecting, and Tweet explains, "He was a damn crazy man—crazy for black women" (*Can't Quit* 4). Cornelia's initial reaction is to discredit Tweet's assertion: "You mean he got after you down *there*—at the cafe? No" (4). But Tweet affirms her characterization with a specific story: "One night, everybody else is gone, he chases me around the kitchen like he's loony. . . . He's going to rape me. No doubt about it" (9). Tweet was able to fend him off with a meat cleaver and run into the café, where "the light's still on, anybody can see in from the street. That changes things. He's supposed to be respectable" (9). Tweet's story of Jones exposes the hidden oppression, the activity that is hidden from light and respectable eyes, like Cornelia's. When Tweet tells Cornelia about her confrontation with his wife, Cornelia assumes Mrs. Jones's reaction would be complete disbelief. Tweet grins at her assumption and says Mrs. Jones simply explained it away with "he's just *like that*" (10).

Exposing the ugly truth about a café owner like Wayne Jones is one thing, but Tweet moves on to stories exposing the dishonesty of two prominent white men, Mr. Lord, a farmer, and Percy Quinn, a lawyer. Two stories about Mr. Lord show his true nature and explain how Tweet lost her grandfather's land and ended up moving to town. She tells the second part of the story, moving to town, first, explaining to Cornelia that having lost the farm, she and Nig were sharecropping on Mr. Lord's land. One year Tweet got exasperated because they had not gotten their money from Mr. Lord although he had sold the crops. Mr. Lord was delaying the payments even though it was Christmas time, or perhaps because it was Christmas time, to keep Tweet and Nig dependent on him. Since Cornelia earlier mentioned her belief that Mr. Lord was an "honest man," Tweet's story must be something of a shock. When Tweet later tells Cornelia the story of losing her land, she explains that Mr. Lord wanted to buy the land, "Fit right into his, like a slice out of a pie. Would straighten out his line if he could get it" (32). She and Nig, however, wanted to farm it. Mr. Lord then calls Tweet's father, Julius, suggesting that he contest the will that gave Tweet the land.

In explaining how Mr. Lord and Julius use the legal system to break the will, Tweet exposes the dishonestly of Percy Quinn as well. Mr. Lord had to consider Quinn's reputation when asking him to conclude that the will he drew up for Tweet's grandfather was not valid. Mr. Lord convinces Quinn by using Tweet's race: "Can't one lie to a nigra in the same way one lies to a woman or a child—because it's in his interest? Who would dream of telling a child the truth about Santa Claus, a wife the truth about one's necessary sexual arrangements, a nigra the truth about—anything? Nigras, like children and women, simply have to be managed for their own good" (112). Quinn apparently buys Lord's argument and explains to Tweet that "given her grandfather's age and state of health, the will was indefensible" (114). Even the law works against those without power.

***

Tweet and the old men in Gaines's novel regain power by making the hidden public and by exposing injustice, but this power is amplified in both works because the audience for the storytelling is white. Ellen Douglas, in explaining the conception of her novel, suggests this very point:

> Before I started writing it, I began thinking about it as a collection of stories told by a black woman. I had a number of stories that I wanted to use. But then, as I was thinking about how to construct it, the first question I had to think about was who is she telling the stories to and under what circumstances is she telling the stories? And that led me to the invention of a person who would be listening. Would she be telling them at home, to her children, to her employer, to her husband? And I decided she should be telling them to a white woman. And that required me to invent the listener, even if the listener didn't have any part in the action. As soon as Cornelia's character began to take shape, it became not a collection of short stories, but rather a novel about the two women. The first voice was already Tweet's. But then I got interested in the relation between the narrator and the listener, and of course that's what the novel is about. The stories are a means for exploring that relationship and exploring the characters of Tweet and Cornelia. ("I'm in That" 38)

Tweet's stories gain force precisely because she tells them to a white woman, who would never dream that men would attempt to attack women at a job or that "honest" white men would use the law to cheat people out of property. Cornelia represents the person in the street looking in the café windows and seeing only the public, appropriate behavior. Tweet thinks of the stories she tells about the hidden behavior as "gifts" she is giving Cornelia. She, for example, "can't resist giving the gift of Percy Quinn to Cornelia, can't resist watching Cornelia visualize that pleasant office in the secluded purlieus of the Farmers' Bank where all the decisions—all the important decisions—are made" (*Can't Quit* 114). Tweet's obvious pleasure at destroying Cornelia's innocence suggests that the "gifts" are more in the form of giving herself power.

Cornelia in fact seems to be a poor audience for these tales. At every turn in the story she interrupts to express disbelief or to suggest a more positive interpretation. When Tweet finishes the story of Wayne Jones, Cornelia says, "I just don't believe it," although the narrator tells the reader, "But of course she does" (10). Cornelia simply does not want to believe the stories because they question her assumptions about the way the world works. In her world everything is orderly and perfect: "Children with straight teeth and straight backs and straight A's; gleaming silver, polished mahogany and walnut surfaces; towels and sheets in ribbon-tied stacks on the shelves" (11). Although she listens to Tweet's tales to be polite, she does not want the larger truths contained in them about racism and oppression to enter her life. She, instead, "accepts the tales like the flowers she sticks in the jelly glass and sets in the window by the kitchen sink and forgets" (14). Tweet in fact subtly points out Cornelia's passivity in making a comparison to Mrs. Lord in her story about Mr. Lord not paying Tweet the money he owed. When Tweet goes to the house to collect it, Mrs. Lord tries to ignore the conflict and to concentrate on the Christmas cookies she is making with her grandchildren. Tweet explains, "She's like you. Always polite. Like to cook. Makes an excuse if she ax you to wait on her" (102). The deeper comparison implied here is that Cornelia, like Mrs. Lord, lives in a dream world of cookie making and does not pay attention to the situation of those around her. Politeness is a poor answer to the problem of racism.

Politeness is certainly not the response of the white audience in *A Gathering of Old Men*. The old men gathered at Mathu's house are telling each other stories as a means of building community, and Keith Clark even argues they are the sole audience: "Gaines embroiders a speech ritual that situates black men as the tellers and hearers, irrespective of whites' desires either to hear or silence their stories" (202). The black men are, however, targeting a white audience in telling their stories to Sheriff Mapes. I would argue, against Clark's assertion, that the true power in the storytelling comes from the cross-racial dialogue. The other black men present know the stories and are aware of the oppression faced by their friends. Sheriff Mapes is, like Cornelia in Douglas's novel, unaware of the full extent of their suppressed pain even if he is not actually the innocent that Cornelia is about the way the world works in terms of race and power. By targeting Mapes, the old men are attempting to gain power by constructing a world very different from the one seen by him. Mapes, however, is just as poor an audience in the beginning as Cornelia is for Tweet's stories. He is not sympathetic to the old men and seems more concerned that their actions are causing him to miss his fishing day. His first response is outright violence. He asks his deputy Griffin to bring "one of them" over to him. Griffin selects Billy Washington, "Uncle Billy," and leads the frail eighty-year-old man to Mapes. When Mapes asks Uncle Billy why he is at Mathu's house, Billy barely gets out the words "I kilt him" before Mapes hits him. After Mapes hits him again with no success, he tries the strategy on a couple more old men. Not only does the violence fail, the men and Candy line up in front of Mapes in defiance, with Candy claiming, "I'm next, Mapes" (*Gathering* 71). Mapes then realizes he must let the men talk, to "work out their gall," hoping that once the stories are over, the men will go home and he can arrest Mathu before Fix and his friends show up.

But even as he lets the men tell their stories in turn, he is not a sympathetic audience. He labels their narratives "tall tales" and questions the conclusions they draw (107). When Yank, for example, connects the loss of horses to break to his killing Beau as "the man who took the horse from me," Mapes asks, "You ever heard of progress?" (99). He further questions the connection between the various sad tales they tell and the supposed target of their revenge, Fix: "Fix didn't rise up in the Senate to keep that boy out of Arlington. He never pulled the switch on that electric chair. . . . And you, Ding . . . that woman who poisoned your sister's child was Sicilian, not Cajun. She had nothing to do with Fix" (107). Corrine responds that they used to have the river but "they took it. Can't go there no more" (107). Mapes again questions the logic by claiming, "I can't fish on that river like I used to. You blaming Fix for that, too? Then you blaming the wrong person. He's as much a victim of these times as you are" (108). When Beulah counters by arguing that Fix once did control the river and drowned two little children, Mapes asks her what proof she has that Fix was involved. Her answer suggests one way their constructions of the past differ: "Black people get lynched, get drowned, get shot, guts all hanging out—and here he come up with ain't no proof who did it" (108). Mapes gets tired of waiting on that "gall" to be worked out, and he interjects some sarcasm in his responses. When Coot takes his turn and claims, "I shot him," Mapes answers, "So did my grandmon" (103). And when Reverend Jamison exclaims, "Look down here, Jesus," Mapes suggests, "He's probably on their side" (105). Humor, however, as well as the questions and the violence show that Mapes is not truly listening or appreciating the stories but simply passing the time, hoping to arrest Mathu before the situation erupts.

***

In examining how these two works use oral storytelling, I have traced a shared concern for racial crossing that differentiates them from earlier southern fiction. But the most intriguing similarity in Gaines's and Douglas's depictions of black characters telling ghost stories to white audiences is their use of senses to show the difficulty of crossing racial barriers through language. Douglas uses hearing and Gaines uses sight to show how very far from understanding the stories the white characters are. By depicting their unawareness as a lack of a basic sense, the two authors underscore the deep divide that exists between Mapes and the old men and between Cornelia and Tweet.

For Cornelia, politeness dictates that she appear to be listening when Tweet is talking, but she does not really hear the stories at all. Cornelia is partially deaf, and although she wears a hearing aid, she often turns the volume down when she is weary of Tweet's talking. Instead of facing the explicit sexuality in some of Tweet's stories or the evidence of cruelty or racism, Cornelia shuts them out: "It was as if the tales had washed over Cornelia like small lapping waves, subsiding into themselves and vanishing" (7). Cornelia has to learn not only to listen to the stories but also to hear what Tweet is telling her through the stories. This, however, will require a wholesale reconception of her world. Cornelia has unconsciously used her deafness to construct a perfect but fictional view of the people around her: "Her children, her husband, her closest friends, all are imaginary people" (129). Just as she shuts out Tweet's ghost stories, she allows her family to "drop their voices so that she will *not* hear" (14). Instead of questioning what might be contained in the hidden communications between her husband and children, Cornelia prefers her silent world, where everything is perfect. When Cornelia finds out those utterances did indeed contain secrets her family was keeping from her, her world falls apart.

To describe how first hearing of her family's "conspiracy" affects Cornelia, the narrator tells an "apocryphal tale," yet again a kind of ghost story, of a beautiful young girl skiing across the surface of a lake. When her rope breaks, instead of calmly waiting for the boat to turn and pick her up, she screams in agony that she is caught in barbed wire. The wire turns out to be a "writhing, tangled mass of water moccasins," and before the driver can pull her into the boat, she exclaims, "Wait!" and slips under the water (131). The story aptly depicts the effect of deafness, skiing over the surface of the water, as well as the danger to Cornelia of truly hearing the family's secrets or of facing the implications of Tweet's stories. In reading this scene, Patricia

Yaeger asks if the skier chooses this fate in telling the boyfriend to wait, so as to "[commune] with the water moccasins, [imbibe] their knowledge with their power?" (3). The question, Yaeger argues, that Douglas asks in this story is "*how do you write a story everyone knows but nobody hears?*" (10). Cornelia has not heard Tweet's stories yet, as she has been deaf to the world lurking under the water of her perfectly constructed life, a world where ghosts protect gold and sing songs.

As Cornelia strives to confront that hidden dark world in her nightmarish journey through New York, she stumbles upon a painting in the Modern Museum of Art that further reflects on her deafness to the potential power of language. The painting is Magritte's *L'Assassin menacé*. Although transfixed by the image, Cornelia cannot figure out why it has captured her attention, thinking that the picture of a dead woman, her assassin listening to a phonograph, and two murderers waiting in the shadows to kill him, has nothing to do with her grief over John's death or Tweet's stories or her children's lives. She notices that the phonograph is the center of the picture and "what is painted here is sound," but "what screams to her from the picture is silence" (212). The dead woman has been literally silenced, the two murderers lurking in the shadows are silent, and the three faces peering in the window at the scene are silent. The only sound, then, is the phonograph, but Cornelia thinks that "no one will ever know what music, what voices come from the horn, why the assassin listens so intently, why he has killed the woman, why he is about to be killed" (213). The painting is another construction of a world that Cornelia cannot understand, just as she did not understand Tweet's stories, for the very same reason that the violence and the sheer ugliness of the scene do not exist in her world. The painting suggests, however, that perhaps the snakes are writhing under the waters, as Cornelia notices how "spotless" the room in the picture is, with everything in place, with perhaps even "ribbon-tied stacks of folded sheets" in the closet. Cornelia longs for her old place, as the respectable, distanced one looking in the window, when she imagines herself escaping past the three faces in the window to "see their backs, where the window will be in shadow, the scene inside invisible," but the scene inside has become visible and she is able to hear. She then wonders if her deafness was intentional—"Did I cement together the hammer and anvil and stirrup so that no vibration passed to the nerve? And the nerve. Did I will its atrophy?"—and understands her lack of hearing is not just a physical malady but a mental one (213).

In *A Gathering of Old Men* seeing becomes the metaphor for understanding that hearing is in *Can't Quit You, Baby*. Sheriff Mapes is not able to see or understand the world the way the old men see it. References to seeing and sight run throughout the novel, but Mapes himself starts the conversation about the problem of sight when he questions Uncle Billy. Trying to catch him in a lie Mapes asks Uncle Billy if Candy's car was already at Mathu's house when he arrived. When Uncle Billy answers, "I can't rightly tell," Mapes assumes it is because Uncle Billy cannot see: "You mean you can't rightly see—that's what you mean, don't you, Uncle Billy?" (78). Uncle Billy's response suggests the double meaning of "see," both sight and understanding, when he counters, "Oh, I sees pretty well, Sheriff, pretty well indeed" (79). The tables are turned on Sheriff Mapes later when Johnny Paul uses sight to question Mapes's ability to understand. As the men one by one claim to have killed Beau, Mapes catches on to their plan of thwarting his ability to arrest Mathu and several times says, "I see" (87). Johnny Paul challenges him with "you see what?" (87). Johnny Paul's point seems confirmed when Mapes answers, "I see nothing but weeds" (88). Johnny Paul then asks the others present what they don't see. When Mapes gets impatient with this discussion, Johnny Paul tells him, "You don't see what we don't see" (89). The repetition of "see" and Johnny Paul's use of a double negative here is certainly in part for its comic and sarcastic effect, as Milton Rickels and Patricia Rickels point out, but the use of the double negative also emphasizes Johnny Paul's point (217). It does not cancel out the negative, as it does in formal grammar ("I do not want to not go to the store" means "I want to go to the store"), but emphasizes the absence of the past. Johnny Paul is pointing out that the absence of the past history of the quarters is not even present for Mapes; he does not miss what is not there. Because Mapes is not understanding his point at all, Johnny Paul finally describes specifically what is missing, the people, houses, and even flowers that still exist for him and whose absence demonstrates the lack felt in the present by the old men. The memory is described again as a haunting with images of the past intruding into the present. Because Mapes does not see the ghosts and the absences, he does not understand the haunting that underlies the men's stories.

The importance of sight and its corollary of understanding is emphasized again later in the novel when Charlie, who has returned to Mathu's house and has admitted to killing Beau, is leading the gun battle against Beau's friends led by Luke Will. Dirty Red wants to understand why Charlie is suddenly so courageous and what gave him the strength to come out of hiding. He asks Charlie, "What you seen in them swamps?" (208). Charlie replies, "You seen it too, Dirty. . . . All of y'all seen it" (208). Dirty still does not understand and says, "I'm just here, Charlie. Like all the rest. I didn't see nothing" (208). Charlie's response, "You got it, Dirty. You already got it, partner," shows that the seeing that has given him courage is not an external sense of sight but an internal sense of understanding.

***

With the white audiences figuratively blind and deaf to the stories told by the black characters, how powerful can those storytellers really be? If, as Yaeger argues, you are telling a story everyone knows but no one hears, how do you make that story loud enough for deaf ears? How do the ghosts break through to the present? In these works, despite the vast barriers depicted by the lack of senses, the characters manage some connections through language. Although Mapes "listens" to the stories in the beginning only to placate the old men, it seems some of their meaning has penetrated his gruff exterior. When Charlie returns from his hiding place in the swamps and confesses to Mapes that he indeed was the one who killed Beau, he asks the sheriff to call him "Mr. Biggs" instead of his nickname, "Big Charlie" (187). In taking the power to choose his name, Charlie shows his newfound courage, telling Mapes: "I'm a man" (187). Mapes's response shows the change in his attitude: "At this point, anything you say . . . Mr. Biggs. That goes for the rest of y'all around here" (187). That he is not being sarcastic now is noted by Lou, who comments, "He was serious, too; he wasn't winking" (188). Charlie then tells the first true story about how Beau was killed, and Mapes is attentive, even "respectful" (189). After the story, Mapes escorts Charlie out of the house, calling him "Mr. Biggs" "with sincerity" (193). Lest the reader gets too caught up in what seems briefly like an idealized moment of understanding, the voice Mapes and Charlie hear when they walk out the door is Luke Will's calling out, "Hand him over, Mapes" (193).

The ensuing gun battle seems to question the success of the storytelling; language does not solve the conflict and the situation still erupts into violence. The problem is rooted in audience; the storytelling may have affected Mapes, but Luke Will and his friends have not heard the stories, and, from the depiction of their glee at a chance to inflict violence, they would not care about the stories anyway. Their focus is solely on the present unanswered murder of their friend. Critics have seen the battle as a problem in the book because it deflates the power the men gained through storytelling. William Mallon argues, "The men's central vehicle for proving their masculinity is language, not violence, the utterance, not the physical act" (50). Suzanne Jones, also concerned with the construction of masculinity, points out the "interesting paradox" in the novel about defining manhood: "In order for

Fix's youngest son Gil to be a man, he must refuse to kill the black man who has murdered his brother Beau; in order for each old black man to be a man, he must be ready to kill a white man" (47). Both of these critics define the power sought by the men in gendered terms, although this can be questioned by the presence of the women, who do participate in the story-telling, at Mathu's house.[2] Mallon resolves the problem of the violence by deemphasizing the importance of the battle scene: "Violence is not a means by which the men achieve manhood; rather, the gunfight is a result of having already achieved it" (64).

I would argue that the split in audience answers the tension and supposed problem of the novel. The men still have to fight Luke Will and his gang because guns are the only communication that will work with them. What Sheriff Mapes does during this battle scene shows that their communication through language worked with him. While his deputy refuses to face Luke Will, arguing, "I ain't raising my hand against no white folks for no nig-gers," Mapes is the first out the door, getting wounded in the process (*Gathering* 195). Luke Will later calls out to Mapes because he is out of bullets, but Mapes offers no help. By the end of the fight Luke Will and Charlie are both dead. Instead of presenting a problem about how to define and achieve manhood, Gaines is acknowledging a complicated and diverse audience. This is not a fairy tale, where stories work like a charm to banish all of the ghosts.

The breakthrough for Cornelia happens when she is alone in New York away from her family and from Tweet. She walks aimlessly through the city day after day trying to escape her grief over John's death and to face the truth about the fictional nature of the world she has constructed in which everything is perfect. It is here, in her nightmarish wandering, that Tweet's stories finally sink in. She hears Tweet's voice telling the stories and guiding her through the city, most comically telling her where to avoid dog shit. When Cornelia thinks her head will burst, she hears Tweet saying, "I'm too polite to say, but I notice you don't hardly ever ax a question, and some-times *seems* like you're listening—you put on listening—but you ain't. Seems like you think you don't need to ax, don't need to listen, you already got an-swers, or else you don't want to hear none" (*Can't Quit* 194). Tweet, or to be more accurate Tweet's voice, finally points out directly the problem of Cornelia's deafness.

It is Tweet's story of Nig's betrayal that helps Cornelia the most, as she is still coping with John's betrayal in keeping secrets from her. Cornelia starts by trying to remember what Tweet did with her grandfather's money but pauses thinking, "This is heavy. Too heavy" (196). Throughout her experience she has the feeling that she is carrying a body on her back. Not her mother or John necessarily; the body seems more like her conscience questioning her every move. In any case, Cornelia is now fully haunted by the past, fully aware of the ghosts wanting attention. Cornelia then hears Tweet retell the story of Nig's affair with Puddin and says, "And then they . . . I want to *hear* it" (199). Nig takes some of Tweet's money and buys a car so he and Puddin can leave town, but Tweet shows up with a pistol and shoots Nig. At that point Cornelia interrupts, and the narrator wonders, "(Is Cornelia at last going to ask a real question?)" (209). Cornelia does ask a question: "Did you ever forgive Nig for . . . ?" (209). Tweet responds, "Didn't have to forgive him. I shot him, didn't I? After that, no use talking about forgiving" (210). Cornelia, still unsure, pushes a bit more, and Tweet responds with the song lyrics of the title: "Well, I can't quit you baby. Just now and then put you down awhile. . . . Love you, baby, but I sure do hate your ways" (210).

By grasping for the first time the sad dimensions of Tweet's stories, Cornelia starts facing how much of her past life was not real. She then visits the museum and stares at the Magritte painting and later has sex with a stranger. She realizes that even though John is dead she is alive. This prepares her to help Tweet who has had a stroke and cannot talk. Cornelia offers to sit with her during the day and brings a present every day to try to reach the Tweet now seemingly buried inside herself. Their roles have basically reversed. Ann Bomberger finds this reversal problematic. Although she first complains that Tweet's stories help Cornelia: "What is more problematic, however, is Douglas's decision to use the character of an African American housekeeper to emotionally 'save' the white protagonist named Cornelia." When the roles reverse, she ironically complains again, "Literally and metaphorically without a 'voice,' Tweet is trapped in her body by Douglas so that a white knight, Cornelia, can come and save her. This ending is quite problematic, because it is through Tweet's complete physical deterioration that Douglas chooses to prove how truly converted Cornelia is" (18, 26). Bomberger suggests that Cornelia does not have to face a fully realized Tweet in the end or make "restitution for her past treatment of Tweet" (28). But this reading ignores the difficulties Cornelia and Tweet face when the roles are reversed and the conversion Cornelia has indeed made with Tweet's help. When Cornelia first sees Tweet, Tweet shoots her an unmistakable look of hatred and rage. Instead of ignoring it, skiing over the surface, as she once would have done, she acknowledges it. She then tells Tweet stories of her time in New York and her childhood. This ability to tell stories was completely missing earlier, as the narrator claims that for Cornelia "it is almost unthinkable to speak to anyone, even herself, of her feelings, her childhood, her intimate life with her husband, even her children's lives. Such confidences are not simply trashy, dishonorable (an old-fashioned word still very much a part of her vocabulary), for her they are scarcely formulable" (*Can't Quit* 66). Certainly a change on some level has taken place.[3]

***

The two novels depict some success in the communication between African American storytellers and their white audiences, but both writers go further than just depicting storytelling as content in these novels. Both also experiment with form by trying to replicate the dynamics of oral storytelling in written prose. In Gaines's novel, oral storytelling influences the form through the use of multiple narrators, each telling the story with their individual dialects, inflections, conclusions, and views. The experiment in Douglas's novel is quite different in that only one person, a narrator, tells the story, but Douglas uses metafictional comments to cast the narrator as a storyteller making choices and consciously constructing a story. The result of the experiment in both novels is a focus on the construction of the narrative, that is, who speaks and how the story is told, so that the power dynamics of storytelling are written into the text. The replication of oral storytelling requires the reader, as an extended audience for the storytelling, to participate in the process. Form, then, does not simply mirror content; in these texts, it performs it.

The orality inscribed in the written text of *A Gathering of Old Men* is highlighted from the very beginning in the structuring of the novel into sections told by different narrators and the titling of these sections with the dual names of each narrator. Valerie Babb suggests that the two names point to the infusion of the oral and written because the formal name is written and the informal name is oral (114). Once again the crucial choice of names shows the power of language, here the difference between written and oral language. The structuring of the novel by narrators also highlights the effect of oral storytelling on the construction of the novel. The sections differ, according to the narrator, in view, in language, and even in content.

The first narrator is "George Eliot, Jr." or "Snookum," who is the only child narrator. His section certainly underscores the importance of the choice of the narrator for the reader. The reader starts with unawareness; as Babb says, Snookum "is the innocent Adam who has not yet partaken of the fruit of racism" (116). He does not understand the implications of the events he relates, so his view is more centered on how these strange events affect his little world. Beau's death is a distant second in his mind to his concern this particular day about getting in trouble because Toddy had seen him and Minnie "playing mama and papa in the weeds" (*Gathering* 3). Snookum carries out Candy's orders to tell everyone to meet at Mathu's house, but to him the significance is how fast he can accomplish the task, throughout noting that "[I was] spanking my butt the way you spank your horse when you want him to run fast" (6). When Snookum is the storyteller, he takes on the power to tell the story through his particular point of view.

Gaines is also careful in each section to make it appear that the character is telling the story by using the language of that character. In an interview with Marcia Gaudet and Carl Wooten, Gaines explains that it is a process where he decides what to put in dialect to render the character of the original utterance and what to convert to formal written language to make it read better in written form (*Porch* 9). What Gaines describes here is free indirect discourse, defined by Suzanne Fleischman as "neither an interpretation of the character's speech or thought, which implies an evaluating Speaker, nor a direct imitation of the quoted individual's voice; rather, the words or thoughts of the self represented retain all their expressivity without suggesting that their grammatical form was that originally uttered, aloud or silently" (228). The prose does not contain then an obvious narrator, a "speaker" as Fleischman puts it, that conveys the language; instead, the language is inflected with the personality, the "expressivity," of the individual character. Janey, for example, in narrating the second section infuses her rendering of the events with the phrases "Lord, Jesus" and "Help me, Lord Jesus" (*Gathering* 11). Gaines also writes selected phrases in dialect, as when Janey is looking for Miss Bea in the back pasture and says, "Lord, Jesus, I thought to myself, now just s'posing, just s'posing, now, a snake or something come up there and bite that old woman in all them weeds" (11). Although Janey is not speaking in direct quotes, there is still the sense of Janey orally telling this story through the language of "s'posing" and "them weeds."

The narrator of each section determines not just view and language but the very content of that part of the novel. Each narrator's personality affects the choices made about what is told. Lou Dimes, as a newspaper reporter, fills his sections with vivid and precise descriptions and a careful rendering of the action. In describing Mapes's arrival at Mathu's house, for example, Lou relates an image of Mapes as he gets out of his car slowly, "as though he was very tired. He was about my height, six three, six four, but he outweighed me by a hundred pounds at least. He was in his late sixties. He wore a gray lightweight suit, a gray hat, white shirt, and a red tie" (63). It is as if Lou is making mental notes for his newspaper report of the event. Lou's section also carefully details, step by step, Mapes's attempt to use violence on the old men to get them to speak.

Splitting the view into different sections according to narrator might seem like a version of the modernist experiment in point of view.[4] The experiment here, though, is different; the narrative voice is complicated by the inclusion of other characters' stories. Uncle Billy's story about his son, for example, is told within Lou's section. Uncle Billy tells this tragic story to answer Mapes's question of why he would want to kill Beau: "'The way they beat him. They beat him till they beat him crazy, and we had to send him to Jackson. He don't even know me and his mama no more. We take him candy, we take him cake, he eat it like a hog eating corn'" (80). This is Uncle Billy's chance to gain power by exposing the cruelty of Fix, and he does so by telling his story in his own words, which are quoted directly, but his story is contained within Lou's narrative. Rufe's section is the most complicated of all as it contains multiple stories and narrators: Johnny Paul telling the story of what used to be in the quarters, Tucker telling about his brother Silas's murder, Yank telling the story of breaking horses, Gable telling the story of his son's execution, Coot telling about not being able to wear his World War I uniform, and Beulah telling about the two children Fix supposedly drowned. The impact of this layering is that the stories are affected by the narrator who relays them. Uncle Billy's story, for example, would be different, if told in a section narrated directly by Uncle Billy. Because it is embedded in Lou's section the story is colored by Lou's viewpoint. Interspersed between Uncle Billy's story and his discussion with Mapes are Lou's descriptions of Uncle Billy with a "swollen bottom lip [that] trembled nervously" and a bald head that "didn't stop bobbing" (81). The image of Uncle Billy as old and frail underscores the pathos of his story of loss. When Mapes orders Uncle Billy to shoot at a bean pole to prove he cannot see, Lou says that "the gun was shaking so much you would have thought it was one of those divining rods that had just discovered water" (81).

In Lou's story of Uncle Billy telling his story we have a listener in effect retelling the story. We have to pay attention not just to the stories the old men tell but how listeners like Lou Dimes and Rufe view the stories. These listeners become tellers when we read the events through their eyes. This move from listener to teller shows the process of oral tradition, where stories are not static but retold, passed around and down. In summoning the courage to tell these repressed stories publicly and hoping for a sympathetic audience, the men seek this very kind of exchange. They want their friends to understand their loss, they want Sheriff Mapes to see the world as they do, and they want the larger world, represented by Lou Dimes, the newspaper reporter, to comprehend their desire for retribution for past crimes. Oral storytelling gives them power because of its potential to be ongoing; unlike written prose that is static and finalized, oral stories can, like Uncle Billy's story, be retold.

When the listeners exchange their roles and become tellers, the reader becomes involved in the process as he or she figuratively becomes the second audience for the storytelling. Tucker may be telling the men gathered at Mathu's house, specifically Sheriff Mapes, the story of his brother Silas, but Rufe tells the reader the story of Tucker telling this story to Mapes. Some sections contain verbal clues that suggest the direct targeting of the reader. When Cherry describes Jacob's actions in the graveyard of pulling weeds off of his sister's grave, Cherry stops his narrative before the shocking story of her burial to speak directly to the reader: "But listen to this now" (45). Tee Jack also speaks directly to the reader when he narrates the events in his bar the afternoon after Beau's murder. He first explains how he knew something was wrong because Charlie did not show up at the mill on time, but realizing the audience might need more information, he says, "Wait–hold it–let me tell you how that worked now" (155). These verbal interjections suggest another audience for the stories, a constructed listener/reader who is now involved.

The reader's inclusion as an audience is further enhanced by Gaines's selection of narrators. The central characters involved in the action of the story–Candy, Mathu, Sheriff Mapes, Fix, Gil, Charlie, and Luke Will–do not narrate a section. The narrators are, instead, the secondary characters such as Lou Dimes and Rufe, who, although involved in the action, are more observers, which makes their point of view closer to the reader of the text, who is necessarily an observer trying to identify the motives of the main actors. This selection of narrators also suggests that the plot is not the central focus of the book. Although the basic plot runs a who-done-it motif with Sheriff Mapes tracking down the killer, the focus is on the stories the men tell about their past, which are at times only tangentially related to the murder of Beau. The choice of narrators, who are observers of the action, shows a focus on the construction of the story instead of the plot or action of the story.[5]

With the reader included as an audience, the potential exists for more retellings of the stories. Stories previously hidden can now become public, and the powerful moment of storytelling is amplified. The prospect for this gathering to have future implications is signaled by the characters when they each touch Charlie as he lay dying, hoping, as Dirty Red tells the reader, "that some of that stuff he had found back there in the swamps might rub off on me" (210). The narrative is possibly just beginning. The last chapter of the novel describes one retelling that occurs just two days later when each of the old men testifies at trial. The storytelling affects the narrative form by suggesting the possibility of future retellings thereby extending the story beyond the written page to include the reader.

A focus on the construction of the narrative and the inclusion of the reader are typical of postmodern works and show that Gaines, writing in the 1980s, is certainly a product of his time.[6] What separates his writing from that of other postmodernists, such as Thomas Pynchon or John Barth, is that the experimentation comes from his use of oral storytelling.[7] As southern writers did before him, he plays with the trope of oral storytelling and uses it to obtain certain effects important in his contemporary time period, specifically cross-racial dialogue. What links his novel to Douglas's is that source of oral tradition. Douglas experiments with storytelling, and her novel becomes postmodern through the use of metafiction, which means fiction commenting on itself. In postmodern works, this usually happens through a narrative voice questioning how a story is told or pointing out alternative versions. In Douglas's novel, this metafiction is rooted in multiple levels of oral storytelling.

As Tweet is telling Cornelia the various stories from her life, the narrator is telling the story of Tweet and Cornelia to the reader, providing a frame to the storytelling. That sections of the prose are at the primary level of Tweet talking to Cornelia is signaled through free indirect discourse; Douglas uses free indirect discourse to suggest that the ideas, voice, and language are Tweet's if not the actual words in a direct quote. For example, the first time Tweet talks to Cornelia is when Tweet tells her the story of Wayne Jones. When the prose becomes free indirect discourse, the use of dialect and fragments suggests its existence as an oral form: "Yeah, he was after me, she says. I was good-looking then. Didn't get these bad risings scarred my face until I was nearly thirty. My skin was smooth. Never did have good hair, but you got to admit even now I got good legs. And I always had these unusual eyes. Make people look twice" (*Can't Quit* 7). Just as Uncle Billy's story is embedded in Lou Dimes's story, a narrator tells the reader the story of Tweet telling Cornelia her story. When the novel shifts to this second level of storytelling, the prose clearly changes: "Tweet has large eyes with long lashes. The irises are two-colored—concentric circles, the inner blue-black, the outer a pale blue—and the white is not white, but faintly tinged with a blue as pure as the sky" (7).

Douglas uses the two levels of storytelling to present Cornelia and Tweet and their stories as simply constructions that could easily be different. The narrator makes metafictional comments showing alternatives to the storyline being presented. After the sorting out of what names the two will use for each other and the positions they hold, the narrator instructs the reader, despite the obvious racial tension underlying the choice of "housekeeper" over "servant," to "try for now to be absentminded about race and class, place and time, even about poverty and wealth, security and deprivation" (5). The narrator, later identified as a "she," then lists "some situations that will not be explored," including Cornelia taking Tweet to register to vote "under the perilous circumstances of black registration in Mississippi in nineteen sixty-four" and Cornelia and Tweet listening to news of Kennedy's assassination on the radio. By showing alternatives to the narrative she does tell, the narrator emphasizes the constructed nature of that narrative. Instead of truly eliminating the alternative stories by claiming they will not be told, the narrator allows them to exist as possible stories, possible alternative constructions if, for example, Cornelia were enough of a civil rights activist to accompany Tweet to register to vote. The effect of pointing to alternative versions is much like Johnny Paul's argument to Sheriff Mapes that what you do not see is as important as what you do see, an argument basically for deconstruction. The narrator emphasizes that she has choices to make in telling the tale of Tweet and Cornelia, and those choices have consequences. When she moves, for example, from the story of Tweet's childhood with her grandfather to Cornelia's childhood, she pauses and wonders how best to encapsulate Cornelia's childhood with a story: "Should I choose sixteen as the illustrative age? No. Begin when she is nine" (40).

The sense that Tweet and Cornelia are constructions is further amplified by the narrator's use of fairy tales. John and Cornelia's meeting is described as a fairy tale with John spotting Cornelia in her tower brushing her hair. He tells her he was walking through the city looking at old houses, as he did in England when he went to see castles, and "saw you sitting in the tower window . . . brushing your hair like Rapunzel" (77). Cornelia continues the thread by suggesting he might need to climb up, if her mother had anything to say about their relationship. Although Cornelia is joking, John does end up rescuing Cornelia from that very tower after her mother, playing the part of the wicked witch, locks her in. The overlay of the fairy tale points to the power of a narrative to shape events; John and Cornelia, as the narrator tells the reader, see their meeting as a fairy tale, and thus the narrator constructs the story to fit the conventions of a fairy tale. The narrator also, however, deconstructs her story with fairy tales by exposing holes in their telling. When she is narrating the story of Tweet telling about Julius's attempt to murder her and her grandfather, the narrator wonders about Julius's motives and how he came to the place where he would be willing to kill his father and daughter. As an explanation, she uses the fairy tale characters Hansel and Gretel, whose father abandoned them to die because the family was poor. But the narrator then deconstructs the story by asking what is not told: "Children who hear the story never ask: What kind of father would do such a dreadful deed?" (51). If Tweet is Gretel with that "kind of father" and a wicked stepmother, the narrator suggests that "she doesn't know, any more than Gretel did, why her daddy and Claree are what they are. She only knows, as she said to Cornelia, that there is evil out there. Inside or outside, it's all the same" (52). The narrator then questions the happy ending that is conventional in fairy tales when she imagines that Tweet will not take her witch's gold home to her father and stepmother. Her life is not a fairy tale, but the fairy tales show that her stories as well as Cornelia's are, indeed, stories, to be constructed any number of ways.

The levels of storytelling in the novel get more complex, however, as the author "Ellen Douglas" exposes the narrator as a construction also. She explains, "She begins, as every storyteller does, with the illusion of freedom. Whose story will she choose to tell? It's her prerogative to decide" (38). "She" could even pick another voice to "hide behind. A man, perhaps. An author who is a black lawyer with an extra Ph.D. in psychology. Or a soft-voiced, steely-eyed black grandmother. Or an elderly single aunt of Cornelia's who is wise and dispassionate. But I would still be here, wouldn't I?" (38). The "I" as opposed to the "she" exposes not just the narrator as a construct but the author as one as well; "Ellen Douglas," is, interestingly enough, a pseudonym, yet another construction for the person named Josephine Haxton.[8] Douglas plays with these metafictional comments to make the reader conscious of the teller, exposing the puppet's strings as it were. The narrator reminds the reader throughout the book of her presence and role in constructing the story. When Cornelia walks through New York hearing Tweet's voice, the narrator interrupts the plot to remind the reader, "But what I want to add, what I want to say now is that *I* am here, too, I, the tale-teller, to warn you, as I have before, that I have a stake in the story. It is not only of Cornelia and Tweet that one must say: Your lives have become so entangled that you can never separate them. Not of them only" (215). In admitting that she has a stake in the story, the narrator reveals that her constructions are not objective and neutral; she is somehow involved, although what stake she has remains concealed, and the reader must be aware that the story is not presented in a vacuum but by an interested person. The interest is in part exposed as a closeness to Cornelia over Tweet. Late in the work, the narrator suggests that she is troubled that perhaps she has been skiing over the complexities of Tweet's life, by only showing Tweet telling stories to Cornelia, and wonders, "What tangle of snakes have I been skiing over?" (240).

In addition to the narrative voice and Tweet's voice, the most complicated section of the book, Cornelia's wanderings through New York, also includes a mysterious disembodied voice, perhaps even a ghost that adds yet one more

layer to the storytelling employed in the novel. The section is already complicated because although Tweet is ostensibly talking, it is not Tweet herself, but
Cornelia's memories of Tweet's stories and her imagination of what Tweet
would say. As in A Gathering of Old Men, this section shows the exchange
of oral storytelling when the listener becomes the teller. In addition to the
Cornelia/Tweet shared voice is a voice of what is described as a body that
Cornelia is carrying. Tweet asks if it is Cornelia's mother because the voice
speaks like a racist woman, but Cornelia says, "No, it's not . . . not Mama"
(194). Since she is carrying the body/voice on her back like a burden, the
voice seems ghost-like, although not connected to a particular person like her
mother or John. It is best described as more generally her past, or perhaps, as
William Dalessio argues, her conscience (105). In order to remember and retell Tweet's story, Cornelia has to ignore the rude interruptions of this voice.

The complications of the various levels of storytelling presented in the
novel act in the same manner as the disjointed and incomplete narratives of
other postmodern works do in necessitating the reader to do some work to
sort out the story and analyze the constructions. The inclusion of the reader
is signaled in the text, as in Gaines's novel, by direct addresses and the use
of the second person. In the second layer of storytelling, the narrator speaks
directly to the reader, as if he or she were present listening to the story being told orally. For example, after pointing out the stories that will not be
included about Cornelia and Tweet, the narrator says, "Try to be absentminded about all these neglected possibilities. You can't? You point out that
by listing them I've included them? Ah, well, I didn't say it was possible. I
said, *Try*" (*Can't Quit* 5). The text here not only includes the reader with the
use of "you" but imagines a reader who interrupts and questions the narrator. Douglas shows the postmodern concern for including the reader in
the construction of the story, but she gets to this concern through her depiction of the exchange of storytellers and their listeners in the dynamics of
oral storytelling. This inclusion has larger implications because of the racial
crossing at the heart of the novel's exploration of these two characters.[9] If
the process of storytelling continues, the listener, now the reader, will then
become a narrator and retell, or at the very least respond to, the haunting
underlying the stories of racism and loss.

***

After giving their readers complicated depictions of how storytelling might
cross racial boundaries, Gaines and Douglas both choose relatively happy
endings. In A Gathering of Old Men, Fix does not "ride" to Mathu's house

and seek revenge for his son Beau's death because his other son, Gil, who is famous as the "salt" of the "salt and pepper" combination of football players at LSU, begs him not to repeat the past in a day when race relations have, in his eyes at least, changed. Although Beau's friends, led by Luke Will, do show up for a fight, the old men repulse them with only Luke Will and Charlie, the two key combatants, dying. The trial resulting from the fight is comical, as the old men tell their stories of the big battle; Lou Dimes tells the reader that "the people passing by out on the street must have thought we were showing a Charlie Chaplin movie" (213). The judge sentences the old men to probation, forbids them to carry guns, and sends everyone home. The old men were able to make their stand and have their day without suffering too many negative effects. In *Can't Quit You, Baby* Cornelia and Tweet finally confront the tension underlying their relationship when Tweet learns to talk again. When Cornelia asks Tweet why she stole a gold barrette of hers and kept it in a bowl, Tweet admits that she has always hated Cornelia and needs the gold barrette to remind her because "sometimes I forget" (254). Cornelia accepts this opinion, claiming to hate Tweet too, but then puts the barrette back into the bowl, seeming to accept the larger reasons Tweet would hate her as a white woman. They also seem to forgive each other as the book ends with Tweet singing, "I love you, baby, but I sure do hate your ways. She's laughing and singing at the same time. I say, I love you, darlin, but I hate your treacherous low down ways" (256). Despite hating the "ways," Tweet has chosen to love Cornelia, much as she forgave Nig earlier and explained, "Can't quit you, baby."

The happy endings in both books, however, are not an easy way out of a complicated and tense exchange between races. Things are not, that is, simply back to normal. The stand the old men take will leave lasting impressions on their larger context. Sheriff Mapes and Candy, who hear the stories firsthand, are changed. Candy has had to give up her protective role toward the men when they defy her and make the decision to stand against Luke Will without her. That Lou Dimes narrates the last section of the book suggests that, as a newspaper reporter, he will report and thus retell the story. Finally, Gil's stand against his father proves that his argument that race relations have changed is valid. Instead of carrying on his family's tradition of racism, he chooses to play with Cal and become, significantly, an "All-American." By admitting her hatred of Cornelia, Tweet acknowledges the effect of oppression on her life. The target of her hatred is described in larger terms: "I hate you all my life, before I ever know you. When you making them Christmas cookies in Mrs. Lord's kitchen, when you saying to me about Wayne Jones: Oh, Tweet, he's just *like* that" (*Can't Quit* 254). By connecting

Cornelia with Mrs. Lord and Mrs. Jones, Tweet shows that what she hates is white oppression; that she sometimes forgets that she hates Cornelia shows the connection these two individuals have made. Cornelia certainly feels the impact of Tweet's admission and links it to Tweet's shooting of Nig: "What can we do, she says, when we've shot somebody?" (256). In both books the past has impacted the present. The ghosts have made their marks.

By using a traditional southern form, oral storytelling, to explore racial crossing, both authors locate that crossing not just in the exchange of language that happens in storytelling, but also firmly in the South. I began this chapter with the suggestion that ghosts haunting the southern landscape are common. I would like to end by asking why this sense of haunting occurs in late twentieth-century southern fiction. In a post–civil rights era when slavery is a distant memory and the machinery of global capitalism is turning the landscape of the South into just another section of postmodern America, why do Gaines and Douglas write about southern ghosts and black ghosts in particular? Why are these ghosts so invested in telling stories?

The easiest of these questions to answer is the question of location; the South is the land of ghosts because it plays a particular role in the conception of American identity. Teresa Goddu in examining the gothic in American fiction explains, "Identified with gothic doom and gloom, the American South serves as the nation's 'other,' becoming the repository for everything from which the nation wants to disassociate itself. The benighted South is able to support the irrational impulses of the gothic that the nation as a whole, born of Enlightenment ideals, cannot" (3–4). The South because of the legacy of slavery carries the burden of the nation's current racial complexities, but in the construction of America as the child of the Enlightenment ideals of equality and freedom, that legacy and burden is hidden, ignored, and repressed. A repressed past intruding on the present finds its perfect fictional emblem in the ghost and its perfect tone in haunting.

The ghosts are figured as black because of the role darkness plays in the literary imagination, as Toni Morrison explains in *Playing in the Dark: Whiteness and the Literary Imagination*: "Explicit or implicit, the Africanist presence informs in compelling and inescapable ways the texture of American literature. It is a dark and abiding presence, there for the literary imagination as both a visible and invisible mediating force" (46). That Africanist presence, though compelling, is hidden in the suppression of stories, such as those of the inhabitants of the cemetery in Gaines's novel. It is a presence that, as Ralph Ellison portrays, becomes invisible, and in its invisibility plays the part of a ghost. In the prologue to *Invisible Man* the narrator explains, "You often doubt if you really exist. You wonder whether you aren't simply a phantom in other people's minds. Say, a figure in a nightmare which the sleeper tries with all his strength to destroy" (4). The white audiences in Gaines's and Douglas's novels do not want to see the ghosts the old men and Tweet see or to hear their stories; their blindness and deafness show their unwillingness to listen to ghost stories.

But Ernest Gaines and Ellen Douglas decide to have their characters tell these ghost stories anyway and to tell these long suppressed stories now. Why now? Toni Morrison's novel *Beloved* is certainly an eloquent argument for the abiding presence and impact of slavery on twentieth-century America and a depiction of that presence specifically as a haunting. And the quote from Houston A. Baker Jr. I began the chapter with suggests that the "ghostly emanations of southern economies of violence against the black body" are still quite potent in their ability to haunt the present. But that Gaines and Douglas are interested in telling these ghost stories is still another issue. Douglas, in her book *Truth: Four Stories I Am Finally Old Enough to Tell*, suggests that enough time has passed from the events she relates, including a massacre of "thirty or more" slaves in 1861, that they can now be told. Perhaps it is only with some distance that the writers can imagine, for example, old men who would rather face lynching at the hands of white racists than run and hide.

Gaines and Douglas both choose to tell the stories of African American characters, but it is in the choice of cross-racial audiences that their books engage in a conversation about language. When Charlie returns to Mathu's house to face the consequences of his killing Beau, he explains that he is now a man: "A man come back. Not no nigger boy. A nigger boy run and run and run. But a man come back" (*Gathering* 187). His image of running suggests that Gaines is explicitly differentiating his depiction of black manhood from the protest tradition of Richard Wright and Ralph Ellison.[10] His novel focuses not on the separation and hiding of the black protagonist but on the conversations between the black men and their white audience about the underlying problems that would cause them to fantasize about murder. For Tweet and Cornelia, it is Tweet's stories exposing the racial boundaries of her world that allow Cornelia to face the mass of snakes existing under the water of the world she has skied across. In both books oral storytelling contains the power needed to effect change. For that change to happen, however, the reader must listen to ghost stories and learn to love despite hating the "treacherous low down ways."

Epilogue

On April 6, 1970, Ralph Ellison published an essay in *Time* magazine entitled, "What America Would Be Like without Blacks." In the essay he claims, "The fantasy of an America free of blacks is at least as old as the dream of creating a truly democratic society" (*Collected Essays* 577). He then traces a historical arc from the early American Colonization Society that wanted to send slaves "back" to Liberia to Daniel Patrick Moynihan's claim that the melting pot did not melt because white citizens resisted assimilation. Although Ellison asserts the idea of "purging the nation of blacks" is "embarrassingly absurd," he admits "the fantasy of a blackless America continues to turn up" (577). Ten years before Ellison's essay, William Melvin Kelley created a fictional world that plays out this fantasy. In his novel, *A Different Drummer*, Kelley constructs an imaginary state, "*bounded on the north by Tennessee; east by Alabama; south by the Gulf of Mexico; west by Mississippi*" (3). Tucker Caliban, the principal African American character in the novel, decides one day to destroy his house and farm, slaughter his livestock, and leave the state without giving any explanation. His silent but profound rejection of society starts a mass exodus of African Americans from the state. The African Americans do not stage a revolt or overthrow the government; they just leave. At first the white citizens simply watch in amazement. The owner of a small country store near Caliban's farm retells the story of Caliban's grandfather, a ferocious African slave who was never broken; the story is offered as a way of explaining Caliban's radical action. Both Caliban's and his grandfather's actions are the exact opposite of assimilation. After a while the white citizens lose their complacency at the loss of the black population, and the book ends with a lynching scene, as the white men try to assert their power through violence. Without African Americans, the white men in Kelley's book struggle to retain their very identities. Kelley's book contains the same conclusion as Ellison's essay: that America would not be America without the presence of African Americans because American identity depends upon the racial divide.

In thinking through the hypothetical idea of what America would then be, Ellison does not focus on what evils would be avoided if we could rewind the tape and start again in an Eden without slavery. He explores what riches would be lost. He points to the loss of American language; "Whether it is admitted or not, much of the sound of [American] language is derived from the timbre of the African voice and the listening habits of the African ear. So there is a de'z and do'z of slave speech sounding beneath our most polished Harvard accents" (*Collected Essays* 581). The language of the African American in "its flexibility, its musicality, its rhythms, freewheeling diction and metaphors, as projected in Negro American folklore" then leads to America's greatest literature, beginning with Mark Twain; "Mark Twain celebrated [the folklore] in the prose of Huckleberry Finn; without the presence of blacks, the book could not have been written. No Huck and Jim, no American novel as we know it. For not only is the black man a co-creator of the language that Mark Twain raised to the level of literary eloquence, but Jim's condition as American and Huck's commitment to freedom are at the moral center of the novel" (581). Without Twain, Ellison writes, then we have no Faulkner, no Crane, and no Hemingway.

Ellison then turns from literary history to examine political history. The political system of the United States derives from the "snarl of forces" that existed from slavery, the Civil War, and Reconstruction (582). Ellison concludes that the "true subject of democracy is not simply material well-being, but the extension of the democratic process in the direction of perfecting itself" (582). The expansion of democracy is, however, difficult. In America's search for identity, white Americans have, according to Ellison, used black Americans as "a marker, a symbol of limits, a metaphor for the 'outsider'" (583). Toni Morrison makes a similar point when she argues that freedom in America actually needed its counterpart in the unfree: "What was distinctive in the New [World] was, first of all, its claim to freedom and, second, the presence of the unfree within the heart of the democratic experiment—the critical absence of democracy, its echo, shadow, and silent force in the political and intellectual activity of some not-Americans. The distinguishing features of the not-Americans were their slave status, their social status—and their color" (*Playing* 48). Morrison's explanation of the necessity of the unfree to set apart and establish the free helps to explain the impulse to fantasize about an America free of blacks. The Other is necessary to establish what an American is not, but the presence of that Other serves as a constant reminder that freedom is limited, incomplete, and even tragic. The Africanist presence both props up the definition of the "American" and diminishes it in the same gesture.

That distinguishing racial color of not-Americans, as Morrison points out, remains a visual marker for the cost and limits of freedom. If America's touted distinction is supposed to be freedom and the Africanist presence questions that freedom, it then becomes easier when thinking of America's cultural distinctiveness to ignore the African American role in creating that culture despite the impact on Twain, Faulkner, Crane, Hemingway, and the American novel as we know it. Ellison argues that this is indeed what happens, rendering African Americans and their influence on the wider American culture invisible: "Few Americans know who and what they really are. That is why few of these groups—or at least the children of these groups— have been able to resist the movies, television, baseball, jazz, football, drum-majoretting, rock, comic strips, radio commercials, soap operas, book clubs, slang, or any of a thousand other expressions and carriers of our pluralistic and easily available popular culture. It is here precisely that ethnic resistance is least effective. On this level the melting pot did indeed melt, creating such deceptive metamorphoses and blending of identities, values and lifestyles that most American whites are culturally part Negro American without even realizing it" (*Collected Essays* 580). Certainly scholars writing after Ellison's 1970 essay have traced the influence of African Americans on the larger American culture, but there is more work to do. By examining oral storytelling my study points to one specific way to trace the blending of cultures. The oral storytelling in the works of the eight writers in this study simply would not be possible without the sharing of culture across racial lines. By putting these writers in conversation, we can see the "blending" that Ellison asserts, although by naming it "confluence," we can see that sharing happens in both directions across the race line. When Ellison points to the importance of the African presence at the very basic level of language, he sets the groundwork for the impact of cross-racial influence in everything embedded in that American language. I have traced some of the direct connections, such as between Joel Chandler Harris and Charles Chesnutt, but the deeper connections that occur from American writers, white and African American, breathing the same air and using the same words is even more profound. When writers shape those words into dialect, into jokes, and into stories, they are dipping their pens into a complicated confluence of cultures, whether they are conscious of it or not.

That we can trace the confluence of cultures in oral storytelling is no accident. The folktales in Harris and Chesnutt, the gossip in Faulkner and Hurston, the jokes in Ellison and Welty, and the ghost stories in Gaines and Douglas exist as written forms on the pages of the novels, but they carry the residue of their existence as products of stories that are shared, from slaves telling stories to Harris as a boy to an African American housekeeper telling stories to her white employer. These eight writers not only draw from a shared pool of stories, they also exchange strategies for making the written stories still seem oral so that they can retain that residue of a former life as live performance. The strategies employed—using creative spelling to mimic dialect, including characters who interrupt the teller and act as stand-ins for a live audience, inserting multiple narrators who tell competing versions of a story, or employing narrators who offer the reader a choice of storylines— are all sophisticated devices that have to be carefully crafted to give the illusion of life to words on a page, the illusion of performance to texts written decades before, the illusion of contingency. When the craft works, as it does in these fine novels, the texts exist somewhere between the written and the oral, and the written words can retain a trace of the open dynamic from the oral storytelling. In oral storytelling the possibility always exists for a new teller of the tale, a different audience to hear it, and perhaps, even in a moment of confluence, an exchange of races. Because oral storytelling is dynamic and ever changing, the next version of the story then changes all the versions that came before it, just like those strings of energy, dancing and intertwining yet again.

Notes

Introduction: Intertwining Strings

1. Marrs reports this as Welty's reaction (*Eudora Welty* 98).

2. My approach is similar to that of Fetterly and Pryse in their study of regionalism and women's writing. They argue that regionalism is a "site of a dialogical critical conversation" and that "as both a literary and a political discourse, regionalism thus also becomes the site of contestation over the meaning of region, one that reveals the ideological underpinnings of regionalization" (2, 6).

3. Bauman has identified a link between reader response and the dynamics of oral storytelling (113).

4. Erlich explains in the 1969 book that *skaz* "does not have any adequate counterpart in English nomenclature bearing on prose fiction" (75).

5. In coining the word "speakerly," Gates is playing off of Roland Barthes use of "readerly" and "writerly" to delineate different kinds of texts.

6. See Irwin for more on this history.

7. See Ayers and Onug; Brown; Steiner and Wrobel; and Wilson.

Chapter 1

1. See, for example, Baer.

2. Irwin examines the frame tale genre from its medieval beginnings and explains that the frame tale "falls into this area that we are still struggling to identify and analyze." She suggests that it "provides a means of textualizing the oral tradition" (32).

3. See Brookes 26.

4. For a completely positive view on Harris's views on race, see Nelson.

5. I refer to this collection of stories as *The Conjure Woman* in this chapter

because that is the original title Chesnutt gave his work, although the edition I am using includes other works and uses the title *The Conjure Tales*.

6. Lynn explains that the function of the frame device in the stories of the southwestern humorists is to keep the "first-person narrators outside and above the comic action, thereby drawing a *cordon sanitaire*, so to speak, between the morally irreproachable Gentleman and the tainted life he described" (64). John Anderson complicates Lynn's reading by disputing the class distinction Lynn sees in the separation between the gentlemen in the frame and the lower-class characters in the story. Anderson sees southwestern humor as making fun of everyone.

7. Douglass explains an analogous situation in the slave songs. Northerners might imagine that slaves were happy when they sang, but they were expressing their sorrow in a way that was veiled enough to be acceptable (75).

8. Baker, for example, points out, "When the work concludes, Julius has obtained a job, use of a building on the Ohioan's property for black community organizational purposes, employment for his grandson, and (possibly) profits from a duplicitous horse trade. In a sense, one might say that Julius has secured—in the very heart of the country districts—an enclave in which a venerable Afro-American spirit can sound off" (*Modernism* 45).

9. MacKethan suggests that "while Uncle Julius may seem to be the traditional darky defender who upholds the assumptions and values of his white masters, what he really does is to destroy the foundations of those assumptions by taking a hard, unromantic look at the way things really were on the black man's side of the fence" (96).

10. Bell discusses the analogous situation of Harris and Twain and their use of older black men to befriend fatherless young white boys.

11. Martin argues that throughout the stories Chesnutt transforms the image of the planter from "benevolent, well-mannered planter patriarch" to "an image characterized by violence, lust, avarice, duplicity, and gullibility" (68).

Chapter 2

1. For Morrison's comments connecting paradise and exclusion, see Farnsworth.

2. See Smith and Lewis.

3. See Naylor for Morrison's comments in 1985 about not having read Zora Neale Hurston until after she began to write (589–90).

4. See Donlon; Bauer, "Sterile New South."

5. Cooper makes this exact argument in reference to Hurston.

6. See Kaplan and Bernard.

7. Makowsky compares Sutpen's design to Plymouth Plantation in terms of the attempt to provide refuge, and the "intolerance and ethnocentricity doom the new Eden" (198).

8. Certainly his being French may also point to a connection to the Old World. Ladd argues that the architect provides a connection between the Old World and New: "In so many ways the slave culture that the Anglo planter in the Deep South inherited (if not the slave culture he envisioned) was established upon a West Indian—predominately French and Spanish—foundation" (143).

9. Kuyk argues that critics have in fact misread Sutpen's design. He claims that Sutpen acquires all the elements of the white plantation owner, so that he could embrace the "nameless stranger" who knocks on the door and thus "he could turn [his dynasty] against dynastic society itself" (204). While this reading might in some small part ameliorate the negative feelings of readers who contemn Sutpen's ruthlessness, it does not change Sutpen's actions when he does gain the dynasty.

10. Donlon sees the porch as a transitional space between public and private where community is formed in one of the few comparisons between these two novels.

11. For further discussion on how Faulkner's gothic house is influenced by Poe, see Coss.

12. As Bollinger explains, "The problem Sutpen evinces, then, is the myth of the autonomous individual. He desires one version of the antebellum American Dream: a plantation, slaves, heirs—and he seems wholly unconscious of the degree to which his success demands collaboration" (213).

13. Levins for example, argues that each of the four narrators uses a different literary genre: Gothic, Greek tragedy, chivalric romance, and the tall tale.

14. See also Awkward and Callahan.

15. Cullick argues that Thomas Sutpen's poor storytelling is connected to his loss of power: "Sutpen's inability to maintain his patriarchal design is a reflection of his inability to maintain a narrative design" (48).

16. The rhetorical contest Jim and Dave conduct for the attention of Daisy also finds it way in the play, *Mule Bone*, written by Hurston and Langston Hughes. Bass, in his introduction to an edition of this play, explains that Hurston and Hughes adapted the plot of the play from a folktale, "The Bone of Contention," which Hurston heard in Eatonville. See Bass for more information on the play and the dispute that caused it not to be finished or produced.

17. Davie explains, "Hurston's text plays with, teases, and fools readers, who expect a story about talking buzzards to be labeled a fiction: Hurston does not oblige. Instead she makes readers uncomfortable with a tale that knocks the props out from underneath the categories of truth and fiction" (452).

18. Ibid.

19. Swink analyzes the actual stylistic devices Faulkner uses that "create an il-lusion of oral quality when one reads it silently" (183).

20. Lazure examines in more depth Rosa's relationship to her audience, Quentin, claiming that Rosa is pursuing a "literary motherhood."

21. See, for example, Brooks, Gray (*Writing*), Matlack, Miller, and Porter.

22. Pitavy argues likewise that Shreve "has a function *in* the novel analogous to that of the reader *of* the novel, capable of distancing, hence of comprehension" (192).

23. Ashmawi argues that critics' extreme views on Tea Cake have kept them from seeing him as "three-dimensional."

24. Entzminger argues that the hunt for black blood draws attention away from the homoeroticism.

25. See Sugimori for a discussion of how critics have followed in Quentin and Shreve's footsteps and assumed Bon's racial mixture.

26. As Watson argues, "Caught up in the sheer contagious fun and excitement of joining in Quentin and Shreve's game, of attacking the riddles that lurk at the heart of the Sutpen tragedy . . . we can all too easily overlook the fact that *Absalom*'s greatest mystery is not so much epistemological as practical, ethical: not who did it or why he did it but how to live with the terrible knowledge you have gleaned, how to put that knowledge to best use" (69–70).

27. As mentioned in the introduction of this work, there is a bit of evidence that Faulkner read a least one story by Hurston in a letter he wrote to Eudora Welty, in which he confuses Welty and Hurston, telling Welty he had read her story, "The Gilded Six-Bits." See Crane.

Chapter 3

1. See Jackson 223.

2. See Marrs (*Eudora*) 52–53.

3. Ralph Ellison and Eudora Welty were acquainted. In her biography of Welty, Suzanne Marrs explains that Welty ate dinner at Ellison's apartment in New York City in the early 1940s, an event which impressed Ellison with Welty's openness (*Eudora* 94). Welty later felt the need to decline to be interviewed by Ellison on television in July 1963 because of her fears of hostility that would be aimed not only at herself but also at her ailing mother (304). Welty wrote to Ellison to explain, and Marrs states, "the Welty/Ellison friendship endured" (305).

4. When asked in an interview about the "rather conspicuous absence of Negroes," Welty responded, "There is, all the same, a very telling and essential incident in *Losing Battles* which is told about, that involves a Negro as such" ("The Interior World" 52).

5. Manning also notes the similarity.

6. See Clarke for a fuller discussion of the image of the car in the novel.

7. See, for example, Dietze.

8. See, for example, Wiggins.

9. In the introduction to *Invisible Man*, Ellison says, "I knew that I was composing a work of fiction, a work of literary art and one that would allow me to

take advantage of the novel's capacity for telling the truth while actually telling a 'lie,' which is the Afro-American folk term for an improvised story" (xxii).

10. Houston A. Baker Jr. argues that Trueblood gives up something to tell his story; in donning the mask to appease the appetite of his white audience, Trueblood performs a minstrel show and offers himself as a commodity ("To Move").

11. Ironically Poe himself inverts the symbolic language in *The Narrative of Arthur Gordon Pym* when the text ends with the gothic terror of whiteness.

12. See also Gross and Hinton.

13. Larkin has an interesting counterreading of this passage, arguing since the narrator says he "fears" that he is speaking for "you," he might fear he is speaking the audience's message instead of his own (270).

Chapter 4

1. See Douglas ("Connections" 6) for her comments on Welty; see Douglas ("Interview" 302) for her comments on Faulkner; see Harrison for more on how Douglas's work answers Faulkner's.

2. The gendered nature of the stand in the novel is problematic. The black women present do participate in the storytelling, but when it comes time to decide whether they will stay and fight, the men exclude them from the discussion. TuSmith suggests that the new sense of community here is not perfect and the exclusion of the women "could be attributed to traditional Southern socialization as well as to Gaines's specific objective of writing about black male liberation" (98).

3. James agrees with my assessment of the ending: "Though it might be said that this rewriting takes place in a situation in which Tweet is virtually silenced, I think it also takes place in a situation in which Cornelia is finally needed; she is, for the first time in her life, called on to give emotionally and physically to another person who will not react with ordinary gratitude but who, in fact, resents her very presence" (84).

4. In answering the question of whether he was influenced by *As I Lay Dying*, Gaines responded: "I was not particularly thinking of Faulkner. I had done that in the last story in *Bloodline*, "Just Like a Tree," using multiple points of view. But Faulkner's *The Sound and the Fury* has had its influence on my work. I don't know that I would have ever been able to write from that multiple point of view had I not read Faulkner, but at the time I was writing it I was not thinking of Faulkner" (*Conversations* 188).

5. Gaudet also suggests that the choice of narrators "reinforces the folk storytelling technique of relating communally a shared event" (18).

6. See Hutcheon 40–42, 43–44.

7. Jeannie Thomas writes about the connections between folklore and the dynamics of postmodernism.

8. Petty argues that the experiment here is actually "meta-autobiography" and that "Douglas is exploring elements of her own subjectivity and actively engaging in self-reflection and self-invention" (125).

9. As James argues, "Douglas introduces a narrative voice that invites readers to think about the story in terms of racism in our own notions" (86).

10. See Clark's argument on Gaines's revision of Wright and Ellison.

Works Cited

Anderson, Benedict. *Imagined Communities: Reflections on the Origin and Spread of Nationalism.* New York: Verso, 1991.

Anderson, John Q. "Scholarship in Southwestern Humor—Past and Present." *Mississippi Quarterly* 17.2 (1964): 67–86.

Armstrong, Dianne. "Twain's Jim: Uncle Remus Redux?" *Nineteenth Century Studies* 9 (1995): 65–84.

Ashmawi, Yvonne Mesa-El. "Janie's Tea-Cake: Sinner, Saint, or Merely Mortal?" *Explicator* 67.3 (2009): 203–6.

Awkward, Michael. "'The inaudible voice of it all!' Silence, Voice, and Action in *Their Eyes Were Watching God.*" *Feminist Criticism and Critical Theory.* Ed. Joe Weixlmann and Houston A. Baker Jr. Greenwood, FL: Penkevill, 1988: 57–109.

Ayers, Edward L., and Onug, Peters. Introduction. *All Over the Map: Rethinking American Regions.* Baltimore: John Hopkins UP, 1996: 1–10.

Babb, Valerie Melissa. *Ernest Gaines.* Boston: Twayne, 1991.

Baer, Florence. "Joel Chandler Harris: An 'Accidental' Folklorist." *Critical Essays on Joel Chandler Harris.* Ed. R. Bruce Bickley Jr. Boston: Hall, 1981: 185–95.

Baker, Houston A., Jr. "A Failed Prophet and Falling Stock: Why Ralph Ellison Was Never Avant-Garde." *Stanford Humanities Review* 7.1 (1999): 4–11.

———. *Modernism and the Harlem Renaissance.* Chicago: U of Chicago P, 1987.

———. "To Move without Moving: An Analysis of Creativity and Commerce in Ralph Ellison's Trueblood Episode." *PMLA* 98.5 (1983): 828–45.

———. *Turning South Again: Re-Thinking Modernism/Re-Reading Booker T.* Durham, NC: Duke UP, 2001.

Bakhtin, Mikhail. *Problems of Dostoevsky's Poetics.* Trans. R. W. Rotsel. Ann Arbor: Ardis, 1973.

———. *Rabelais and His World.* Trans. Helene Iswolsky. Cambridge, MA: MIT UP, 1968.

Banks, Ann. *First Person America (For the Federal Writer's Project)*. New York: Knopf, 1980.

Bass, George Houston. "Another Bone of Contention: Reclaiming Our Gift of Laughter." Introduction. *Mule Bone: A Comedy of Negro Life*. Langston Hughes and Zora Neale Hurston. New York: Perennial, 1991: 1–4.

Bauer, Margaret D. "The Sterile New South: An Intertextual Reading of *Their Eyes Were Watching God* and *Absalom, Absalom!*" *CLA Journal* 36.4 (1993): 384–405.

——. *William Faulkner's Legacy: "What Shadow, What Stain, What Mark."* Gainesville: UP of Florida, 2005.

Bauman, Richard. *Story, Performance, and Event*. Cambridge: Cambridge UP, 1986.

Bearden, Kenneth. "Monkeying Around: Welty's 'Powerhouse,' Blues-Jazz, and the Signifying Connection." *Southern Literary Journal* 31.2 (1999): 65–79.

Beavers, Herman. *Wrestling Angels into Song: The Fictions of Ernest J. Gaines and James Alan McPherson*. Philadelphia: U of Pennsylvania P, 1995.

Bell, William R. "The Relationship of Joel Chandler Harris and Mark Twain." *Atlanta Historical Journal* 30.3–4 (1986–87): 97–111.

Benjamin, Walter. "The Storyteller: Observations on the Works of Nikolai Leskov" in *Walter Benjamin: Selected Writings, Volume 3: 1935–38*. Trans. Edmund Jephcott, Howard Eiland, and others. Ed. Howard Eiland and Michael W. Jennings. Cambridge, MA: Harvard UP, 2002: 143–66.

Bergson, Henri. "Laughter." *Comedy*. Ed. Wylie Sypher. New York: Double Day, 1956: 61–190.

Berman, Daniel M. *It Is So Ordered: The Supreme Court Rules on School Segregation*. New York: Norton, 1966.

Bernard, Emily. "The Renaissance and the Vogue." *The Cambridge Companion to the Harlem Renaissance*. Ed. George Hutchinson. New York: Cambridge UP, 2007: 28–40.

Bickley, R. Bruce. *Joel Chandler Harris*. Boston: Twayne, 1978.

Blake, Susan. "Ritual and Rationalization: Black Folklore in the Works of Ralph Ellison." *PMLA* 94.1 (1979): 121–36.

Bold, Christine. *The WPA Guides: Mapping America*. Jackson: UP of Mississippi, 1999.

Bollinger, Laurel. "'That Triumvirate Mother-Woman': Narrative Authority and Interdividuality in *Absalom, Absalom!*" *LIT: Literature Interpretation Theory* 9.3 (1998): 197–223.

Bomberger, Ann M. "The Servant and the Served: Ellen Douglas's *Can't Quit You, Baby*." *Southern Literary Journal* 31.1 (1998): 17–34.

Bone, Robert. *Down Home: A History of Afro-American Short Fiction from Its Beginnings to the End of the Harlem Renaissance*. New York: Putnam's, 1975.

Brigham, Cathy. "The Talking Frame of Zora Neale Hurston's Talking Book: Storytelling as Dialectic in *Their Eyes Were Watching God*." *College Language Association* 37 (1994): 402–19.

Brodhead, Richard H. *Cultures of Letters: Scenes of Reading and Writing in Nineteenth-Century America*. Chicago: U of Chicago P, 1993.

——. Introduction. *The Conjure Woman and Other Conjure Tales*. Ed. Brodhead. Durham, NC: Duke UP, 1993: 1–22.

Brookes, Stella Brewer. *Joel Chandler Harris–Folklorist*. Athens: U of Georgia P, 1950.

Brooks, Peter. *Design and Intention in Narrative*. New York: Knopf, 1984.

Brown, Richard Maxwell. "The New Regionalism in America, 1970–1981." *Regionalism and the Pacific Northwest*. Ed. William G. Robbins, Robert J. Frank, and Richard E. Ross. Corvallis: Oregon State UP, 1983: 37–96.

Busby, Mark. *Ralph Ellison*. Boston: Twayne, 1991.

Callahan, John F. *In the African-American Grain: The Pursuit of Voice in Twentieth-Century Black Fiction*. Urbana: U of Illinois P, 1988.

Carpio, Glenda R. *Laughing Fit to Kill: Black Humor in the Fictions of Slavery*. Oxford: Oxford UP, 2008.

Cassidy, Thomas. "Janie's Rage: The Dog and the Storm in *Their Eyes Were Watching God*." *CLA Journal* 36.3 (1993): 260–69.

Chaplin, Charlie. *My Autobiography*. New York: Simon, 1964.

Chesnutt, Charles W. *Conjure Tales and Stories of the Color Line*. New York: Penguin, 1992.

——. "The Dumb Witness." *The Short Fiction of Charles W. Chesnutt*. Ed. Sylvia Render. Washington, DC: Howard UP, 1974: 153–63.

——. "Post-Bellum-Pre-Harlem." *Crisis* 38 (1931): 191–94.

——. "Superstitions and Folk-Lore of the South." *Modern Culture* 13 (1901): 231–35.

Clark, Keith. "Re-(W)righting Black Male Subjectivity: The Communal Poetics of Ernest Gaines's *A Gathering of Old Men*." *Callaloo* 22.1 (1999): 195–207.

Clarke, Deborah. "Eudora Welty's *Losing Battles*: Cars and Family Values." *Mississippi Quarterly* Supplement 2009: 143–57.

Clayton, Jay. "The Narrative Turn in Recent Minority Fiction." *American Literary History* 2 (1990): 375–93.

Cohen, Hennig, and William B. Dillingham. *Humor of the Old Southwest*. Athens: U of Georgia P, 1964.

Connolly, Paula T. "Crossing Borders from Africa to America." *Transcending Boundaries: Writing for a Dual Audience of Children and Adults*. Ed. Sandra L. Beckett. New York: Garland, 1999: 149–64.

Cooper, Jan. "Zora Neale Hurston Was Always a Southerner, Too." *The Female Tradition in Southern Literature*. Ed. Carol S. Manning. Urbana: U of Illinois P, 1993: 57–70.

Coss, David L. "Sutpen's Sentient House." *Journal of the Fantastic in the Arts* 15.2 (2005): 101–18.

Crane, Joan St. C. "William Faulkner to Eudora Welty: A Letter." *Mississippi Quarterly* 42.3 (1989): 223–27.

Cullick, Jonathan S. "'I Had a Design': Sutpen as Narrator in *Absalom, Absalom!*" *Southern Literary Journal* 28.2 (1996): 48–58.

Dalessio, William, Jr. "*A Lifetime Burning* and *Can't Quit You, Baby*: Acknowledging, Challenging, and Replacing 'Comfortable Lies.'" *Southern Quarterly* 36.1 (1997): 99–106.

Davie, Sharon. "Free Mules, Talking Buzzards, and Cracked Plates: The Politics of Dislocation in *Their Eyes Were Watching God*." *PMLA* 108.3 (1993): 446–58.

Dietze, R. F. "Crainway and Son: Ralph Ellison's *Invisible Man* as Seen through the Perspective of Twain, Crane, and Hemingway." *Delta: Revue du Centre d'Etudes* 18 (1984): 25–46.

Donlon, Jocelyn Hazlewood. "Porches: Stories: Power: Spatial and Racial Intersection in Faulkner and Hurston." *Journal of American Culture* 19.4 (1996): 95–111.

Donnelly, Colleen. "Compelled to Believe: Historiography and Truth in *Absalom, Absalom!*" *Style* 25.1 (1991): 104–22.

Douglas, Ellen. *Can't Quit You, Baby*. New York: Penguin, 1989.

——. "Connections." *Eudora Welty Newsletter* July 2001, 6.

——. "'I'm in That Secular World, Even Though I Keep Looking Around for Someplace Else to Be': Interview with Ellen Douglas." By Betty Tardieu. *Southern Quarterly* 33.4 (1995): 23–39. Rpt. in *Conversations with Ellen Douglas*. Ed. Panthea Reid. Jackson: UP of Mississippi, 2000: 121–39.

——. "Interview with Ellen Douglas: February 25, 1997." By Charline R. McCord. *Mississippi Quarterly* 51.2 (1998): 291–322.

Douglass, Frederick. *My Bondage and My Freedom*. New York: Penguin, 2003.

Duck, Leigh Anne. *The Nation's Region: Southern Modernism, Segregation, and U.S. Nationalism*. Athens: U of Georgia P, 2006.

Ellison, Ralph. "Change the Joke and Slip the Yoke." *Shadow and Act*. New York: Random, 1953: 45–59.

——. *The Collected Essays of Ralph Ellison*. Ed. John F. Callahan. New York: Modern Library, 1995.

——. *Invisible Man*. New York: Vintage, 1995.

Entzminger, Betina. "Passing as Miscegenation: Whiteness and Homoeroticism in Faulkner's *Absalom, Absalom!*" *Faulkner Journal* 22.1–2 (2006–7): 90–105.

Erlich, Victor. *Russian Formalism: History–Doctrine*. 3rd ed. Paris: Mouton, 1969.

Evans, Elizabeth. *Eudora Welty*. New York: Unger, 1981.

Fabre, Michel. "The Narrator/Narratee Relationship in *Invisible Man*." *Callaloo* 8.3 (1985): 535–43.

Farnsworth, Elizabeth. "Conversation: Toni Morrison." *The News Hour with Jim Lehrer*. National Public Radio, 9 March 1998. http://www.pbs.org/newshour/bb/entertainment/jan-june98/morrison_3-9.html.

Faulkner, William. *Absalom, Absalom!* New York: Vintage, 1990.

Fetterly, Judith, and Marjorie Pryse. *Writing out of Place: Regionalism, Women, and American Literary Culture*. Urbana: U of Illinois P, 2003.

Fishkin, Shelley Fisher. *Was Huck Black?: Mark Twain and African-American Voices.* New York: Oxford UP, 1993.

Fleischman, Suzanne. *Tense and Narrativity: From Medieval Performance to Modern Fiction.* Austin: U of Texas P, 1990.

Gaines, Ernest J. *Conversations with Ernest Gaines.* Ed. John Lowe. Jackson: UP of Mississippi, 1995.

——. *A Gathering of Old Men.* New York: Vintage, 1992.

——. *Porch Talk with Ernest Gaines: Conversations on the Writer's Craft.* Ed. Marcia Gaudet and Carl Wooten. Baton Rouge: Louisiana State UP, 1990.

Gates, Henry Louis, Jr. *The Signifying Monkey: A Theory of Afro-American Literary Criticism.* New York: Oxford UP, 1988.

Gaudet, Marcia. "Gaines' Fifteen Narrators: Narrative Style and Storytelling Technique in *A Gathering of Old Men.*" *Louisiana Folklore Miscellany* 6.3 (1990): 15–22.

Glazier, Lyle. "The Uncle Remus Stories: Two Portraits of American Negroes." *Jou nal of General Education* 22 (1970): 71–79.

Gleason, William. "Chesnutt's Piazza Tales: Architecture, Race, and Memory in the Conjure Stories." *American Quarterly* 51.1 (1999): 33–77.

Goddu, Teresa. "The Ghost of Race: Edgar Allan Poe and the Southern Gothic." *Criticism and the Color Line: Desegregating American Literary Studies.* Ed. Henry B. Wonham. New Brunswick, NJ: Rutgers UP, 1996: 230–50.

——. *Gothic America: Narrative, History, and Nation.* New York: Columbia UP, 1997.

Gray, Richard. *A Web of Words: The Great Dialogue of Southern Literature.* Athens: U of Georgia P, 2007.

——. *Writing the South: Ideas of an American Region.* Cambridge: Cambridge UP, 1986.

Greeson, Jennifer Rae. *Our South: Geographic Fantasy and the Rise of National Literature.* Cambridge, MA: Harvard UP, 2010.

Gretlund, Jan Nordby. *Eudora Welty's Aesthetics of Place.* Odense, Den.: Odense UP, 1994.

Griffin, Joseph. "Calling, Naming, and Coming of Age in Ernest Gaines's *A Gathering of Old Men.*" *Names: A Journal of Onomastics* 40.2 (1992): 89–97.

Gross, Seymour. "A Long Day's Living: The Angelic Ingenuities of *Losing Battles.*" *Eudora Welty: Critical Essays.* Ed. Peggy Whitman Prenshaw. Jackson: UP of Mississippi, 1979: 325–40.

Gygax, Franziska. *Serious Daring from Within: Female Narrative Strategies in Eudora Welty's Novels.* New York: Greenwood, 1990.

Harris, Joel Chandler. *Uncle Remus: His Songs and His Sayings.* New York: Penguin, 1982.

Harris, Trudier. *The Storyteller's Craft in Zora Neale Hurston, Gloria Naylor, and Randall Kenan.* Athens: U of Georgia P, 1996.

Harrison, Suzan. "Repudiating Faulkner: Race and Responsibility in Ellen Douglas's *The Rock Cried Out.*" *Southern Literary Journal* 36.1 (2003): 1–20.

Heermance, J. Noel. *Charles W. Chesnutt: America's First Great Black Novelist.* Hamden, CT: Archon, 1974.

Hemenway, Robert. "Author, Teller, and Hero." Introduction. *Uncle Remus: His Songs and His Sayings.* By Joel Chandler Harris. New York: Penguin, 1982: 7-31.

Hinton, Jane L. "The Role of Family in *Delta Wedding, Losing Battles,* and *The Optimist's Daughter.*" *Eudora Welty: Critical Essays.* Ed. Peggy Whitman Prenshaw. Jackson: UP of Mississippi, 1979: 120-31.

Hoffmann, Gerhard. "*Absalom, Absalom!:* A Postmodern Approach." *Faulkner's Discourse: An International Symposium.* Ed. Lothar Honnighausen. Tübingen, Ger.: Max Niemeyer Verlag, 1989: 276-92.

Howard, Lillie P. *Zora Neale Hurston.* Boston: Twayne, 1980.

Humphries, Jefferson. "Remus Redux, or French Classicism on the Old Plantation: La Fontaine and J. C. Harris." *Southern Literature and Literary Theory.* Ed. Jefferson Humphries. Athens: U of Georgia P, 1990: 170-85.

Hurston, Zora Neale. "Characteristics of Negro Expression." *Negro: Anthology.* Ed. Nancy Cunard. New York: Negro UP, 1969: 27-46.

——. *Their Eyes Were Watching God.* New York: Harper, 1937.

Hutcheon, Linda. *A Poetics of Postmodernism: History, Theory, Fiction.* New York: Routledge, 1988.

Irwin, Bonnie D. "What's in a Frame? The Medieval Textualization of Traditional Storytelling." *Oral Tradition* 10.1 (1995): 27-53.

Jackson, Lawrence. *Ralph Ellison: Emergence of Genius.* Athens: U of Georgia P, 2007.

James, Theresa. "Race in the Kitchen: Domesticity and the Growth of Racial Harmony in Ellen Douglas's *Can't Quit You, Baby* and Christine Wiltz's *Glass House.*" *South Atlantic Review* 65.1 (2000): 78-97.

Johns, Gillian. "Jim Trueblood and His Critic-Readers: Ralph Ellison's Rhetoric of Dramatic Irony and Tall Humor in the Mid-Century American Literary Public Sphere." *Texas Studies in Literature and Language* 49.3 (2007): 230-64.

Jones, Gavin. *Strange Talk: The Politics of Dialect Literature in Gilded Age America.* Berkeley: U of California P, 1999.

Jones, Jill. "The Eye of a Needle: Morrison's *Paradise,* Faulkner's *Absalom, Absalom!,* and the American Jeremiad." *Faulkner Journal* 17.2 (2002): 3-23.

Jones, Suzanne. "Reconstructing Manhood: Race, Masculinity and Narrative Closure in Ernest Gaines's *A Gathering of Old Men* and *A Lesson Before Dying.*" *Masculinities* 3.2. (1995): 43-66.

Kaplan, Carla. "The Erotics of Talk: 'That Oldest Human Longing' in *Their Eyes Were Watching God.*" *American Literature* 67.1 (1995): 115-42.

Kelley, William Melvin. *A Different Drummer.* New York: Anchor, 1969.

Klein, Marcus. *After Alteration: American Novels in Mid-Century.* New York: World, 1964.

——. "Zora Neale Hurston, Folk Performance, and the 'Margarine Negro.'" *The*

Cambridge Companion to the Harlem Renaissance. Ed. George Hutchinson. New York: Cambridge UP, 2007: 213–35.

Korobkin, Laura. "Legal Narratives of Self-Defense and Self-Effacement in *Their Eyes Were Watching God.*" *Studies in American Fiction* 31.1 (2003): 3–28.

Kreyling, Michael. *Inventing Southern Literature.* Jackson: UP of Mississippi, 1998.

Kulh, Elon A. "Poetic License and Chesnutt's Use of Folklore." *CLA Journal* 38.2 (1994): 247–53.

Kuyk, Dirk, Jr. "Sutpen's Design." *William Faulkner's Absalom, Absalom!: A Casebook.* Ed. Fred Hobson. New York: Oxford UP, 2003: 189–217.

Ladd, Barbara. *Nationalism and the Color Line in George W. Cable, Mark Twain, and William Faulkner.* Baton Rouge: Louisiana State UP, 1996.

Largent, Charlie. "Popeye the Sailor." *Video Watchdog* 137 (2008): 53.

Larkin, Lesley. "Postwar Liberalism, Close Reading, and 'You': Ralph Ellison's *Invisible Man,*" *LIT: Literature Interpretation Theory* 19.3 (2008): 268–304.

Latham, Sean. "Jim Bond's America: Denaturalizing the Logic of Slavery in *Absalom, Absalom!*" *Mississippi Quarterly* 51.3 (1998): 453–64.

Lazure, Erica Plouffe. "A Literary Motherhood: Rosa Coldfield's Design in *Absalom, Absalom!*" *Mississippi Quarterly* 62.3–4 (2009): 479–96.

Lester, Julius. "The Storyteller's Voice: Reflections on the Rewriting of Uncle Remus." *The Voice of the Narrator in Children's Literature: Insights from Writers and Critics.* Ed. Charlotte F. Otten and Gary D. Schmidt. New York: Greenwood, 1989: 69–73.

——. *The Tales of Uncle Remus.* New York: Dial, 1987.

Levecq, Christine. "'You Heard Her, You Ain't Blind': Subversive Shifts in Zora Neale Hurston's *Their Eyes Were Watching God.*" *Tulsa Studies in Women's Literature* 13.1 (1994): 87–111.

Levins, Lynn Gartrell. "The Four Narrative Perspectives in *Absalom, Absalom!*" *PMLA* 85.1 (1970): 35–47.

Lewis, R. W. B. *The American Adam: Innocence, Tragedy, and Tradition in the Nineteenth Century.* Chicago: U of Chicago P, 1968.

Lowe, John. *Jump at the Sun: Zora Neale Hurston's Cosmic Comedy.* Chicago: U of Illinois P, 1994.

Lynn, Kenneth S. *Mark Twain and Southwestern Humor.* Westport, CT: Greenwood, 1959.

MacKethan, Lucinda Hardwick. *The Dream of Arcady: Place and Time in Southern Literature.* Baton Rouge: Louisiana State UP, 1980.

Makowsky, Veronica. "Noxious Nostalgia: Fitzgerald, Faulkner, and the Legacy of Plantation Fiction." *F. Scott Fitzgerald in the Twenty-First Century.* Ed. Jackson R. Bryer, Ruth Prigozy, and Milton R. Stern. Tuscaloosa: U of Alabama P, 2003: 190–201.

Mallon, William T. "Voicing Manhood: Masculinity and Dialogue in Ernest J. Gaines's 'The Sky Is Gray,' 'Three Men,' and *A Gathering of Old Men.*" *Southern Studies* 5.3–4 (1994): 49–67.

Manning, Carol S. *With Ears Opening Like Morning Glories: Eudora Welty and the Love of Storytelling*. New York: Greenwood, 1980.

Marrs, Suzanne. *Eudora Welty: A Biography*. New York: Harcourt, 2005.

———. "The Making of *Losing Battles*: Jack Renfro's Evolution." *Mississippi Quarterly* 37 (1984): 469–74.

———. *One Writer's Imagination: The Fiction of Eudora Welty*. Baton Rouge: Louisiana UP, 2002.

———. "'The Treasure Most Dearly Regarded': Memory and Imagination in *Delta Wedding*." *Southern Literary Journal* 25.2 (1993): 79–91.

Martin, Gretchen. "Overfamiliarization as Subversive Plantation Critique in Charles W. Chesnutt's *The Conjure Woman and Other Conjure Tales*." *South Atlantic Review* 74.1 (2009): 65–86.

Marx, Leo. *The Machine in the Garden: Technology and the Pastoral Ideal in America*. New York: Oxford UP, 2000.

Matlack, James H. "The Voices of Time: Narrative Structure in *Absalom, Absalom!*" *Southern Review* 15.2 (1979): 333–54.

McHaney, Thomas L. "Faulkner Borrows from the Mississippi Guide." *Mississippi Quarterly* 19 (1996): 116–20.

McPherson, Karen. "*Absalom, Absalom!*: Telling Scratches." *Modern Fiction Studies* 33.3 (1987): 431–50.

Melendez, Theresa. "The Oral Tradition and the Study of American Literature." *Redefining American Literary History*. Ed. A. LaVonne Brown Ruoff and Jerry W. Ward. New York: MLA, 1990: 75–82.

Miller, J. Hillis. "Ideology and Topography in Faulkner's *Absalom, Absalom!*" *Faulkner and Ideology*. Ed. Donald M. Kartiganer and Ann Abadie. Jackson: UP of Mississippi, 1995: 253–76.

Minter, David. *William Faulkner: His Life and Work*. Baltimore: Johns Hopkins UP, 1980.

Mississippi: A Guide to the Magnolia State. American Guide Series. New York: Viking P, 1938.

Morgan, Winifred. "Signifying: The African-American Trickster and the Humor of the Old Southwest." *The Enduring Legacy of Old Southwest Humor*. Ed. Ed Piacentino. Baton Rouge: Louisiana State UP, 2006: 210–26.

Morrison, Toni. "The Art of Fiction: Interview." *Paris Review* 129 (1993): 83–125.

———. *Paradise*. New York: Knopf, 1997.

———. *Playing in the Dark: Whiteness and the Literary Imagination*. Cambridge, MA: Harvard UP, 1992.

Nadel, Alan. "The Integrated Literary Tradition." *A Historical Guide to Ralph Ellison*. Ed. Steven C. Tracy. Oxford: Oxford UP, 2004: 143–70.

———. *Invisible Criticism: Ralph Ellison and the American Canon*. Iowa City: U of Iowa P, 1988.

Naylor, Gloria. "A Conversation: Gloria Naylor and Toni Morrison." *Southern Review* 21 (1985): 567–93.

Nelson, John Herbert. *The Negro Character in American Literature*. Lawrence, KS: Department of Journalism P, 1926.

Oates, Joyce Carol. "Eudora's Web." *Atlantic* 225.4 (1970): 118–22.

Ong, Walter J. *Interfaces of the Word: Studies in the Evolution of Consciousness and Culture*. Ithaca: Cornell UP, 1977.

———. *Orality and Literacy: The Technologizing of the Word*. New York: Rutledge, 1982.

Penkower, Monty Noam. *The Federal Writers' Project*. New York: Columbia UP, 1973.

Petrie, Paul R. "Charles W. Chesnutt, *The Conjure Woman*, and the Racial Limits of Literary Meditation." *Studies in American Fiction* 27.2 (1999): 183–204.

Petty, Leslie. "'She Has Some Buried Connection with These Lives': Autobiographical Acts in *Can't Quit You, Baby*." *Southern Quarterly* 33.4 (1995): 121–29.

Pitavy, Francois. "The Narrative Voice and Function of Shreve: Remarks on the Production of Meaning in *Absalom, Absalom!*" *William Faulkner's Absalom, Absalom!: A Casebook*. Ed. Elizabeth Muhlenfield. New York: Garland, 1984: 189–205.

Porter, Carolyn. "Faulkner and His Reader." *Faulkner and the Unappeased Imagination: A Collection of Critical Essays*. Ed. Glenn O. Carey. Troy, NY: Whitston, 1980: 231–58.

Reed, Joseph W. *Faulkner's Narrative*. New Haven, CT: Yale UP, 1973.

Rickels, Milton, and Patricia Rickels. "'The Sound of My People Talking': Folk Humor in *A Gathering of Old Men*." *Critical Reflections on the Fiction of Ernest J. Gaines*. Ed. David C. Estes. Athens: U of Georgia P, 1994: 215–27.

Rushdie, Salman. "In Good Faith." *Imaginary Homelands: Essays and Criticism 1981–1991*. London: Granta, 1991: 393–414.

Schmidt, Peter. "Command Performances: Black Storytellers in Stuart's 'Blink' and Chesnutt's 'The Dumb Witness.'" *Southern Literary Journal* 35.1 (2002): 70–96.

Seelye, Katharine. "Writer Tends Land Where Ancestors Were Slaves." *New York Times* 20 October 2010: A18.

Sensibar, Judith L. *Faulkner and Love: The Women Who Shaped His Art*. New Haven: Yale UP, 2009.

Skaggs, Merrill Maguire. *The Folk of Southern Fiction*. Athens: U of Georgia P, 1972.

Smith, Henry Nash. *Virgin Land: The American West as Symbol and Myth*. Cambridge, MA: Harvard UP, 1950.

Spaulding, A. Timothy. "Embracing Chaos in Narrative Form: The Bebop Aesthetic in Ralph Ellison's *Invisible Man*." *Callaloo* 27.2 (2004): 481–501.

Steinbeck, John. *The Grapes of Wrath*. New York: Penguin, 1992.

Steiner, Michael C., and David M. Wrobel, "Many Wests: Discovering a Dynamic Western Regionalism." *Many Wests: Place, Culture, & Regional Identity*. Ed. David M. Wrobel and Michael C. Steiner. Lawrence: U of Kansas P, 1997: 1–30.

Stepto, Robert B. *From Behind the Veil: A Study of Afro-American Narrative.* Urbana: U of Chicago P, 1979.

——. "'The Simple but Intensely Human Inner Life of Slavery': Storytelling, Fiction and the Revision of History in Charles W. Chesnutt's 'Uncle Julius Stories.'" *History and Tradition in Afro-American Culture.* Ed. Gunter H. Lenz. Frankfurt: Campus Verlag, 1984: 29–51.

Stroup, Sheila. "'We're All Part of It Together': Eudora Welty's Hopeful Vision in *Losing Battles.*" *Southern Literary Journal* 15.2 (1983): 42–58.

Sugimori, Masami. "Racial Mixture, Racial Passing, and White Subjectivity in *Absalom, Absalom!*" *Faulkner Journal* 23.2 (2008): 3–21.

Sundquist, Eric J. "*Invisible Man:* The Novel of Segregation." *Cultural Contexts for Ralph Ellison's Invisible Man.* Ed. Eric J Sundquist. Boston: Bedford/St. Martin's, 1995: 1–30.

——. *To Wake the Nations: Race in the Making of American Literature.* Cambridge, MA: Harvard UP, 1993.

Swink, Helen. "William Faulkner: The Novelist as Oral Narrator." *Georgia Review* 26.2 (1972): 183–209.

Tate, Allen. "A Southern Mode of the Imagination." *Essays of Four Decades.* Chicago: Swallow, 1959: 577–92.

Thomas, Jeannie B. "Out of the Frying Pan and into the Postmodern: Folklore and Contemporary Literary Theory." *Southern Folklore* 51.2 (1994): 107–20.

TuSmith, Bonnie. *All My Relatives: Community in Contemporary Ethnic American Literature.* Ann Arbor: U of Michigan P, 1993.

Twain, Mark. *The Adventures of Huckleberry Finn.* Berkeley: U of California P, 1985.

——. "How to Tell a Story." *How to Tell a Story and Other Essays.* New York: Oxford UP, 1996: 3–12.

Vernon, Alex. "Narrative Miscegenation: *Absalom, Absalom!* as Naturalist Novel, Autobiography, and African-American Oral Story." *Journal of Narrative Theory* 31.2 (2001): 155–79.

Waldron, Ann. *Eudora Welty: A Writer's Life.* New York: Doubleday, 1998.

Walker, Alice. "The Dummy in the Window: Joel Chandler Harris and the Invention of Uncle Remus." *Living by the Word: Selected Writings, 1973–1987.* San Diego: Harcourt, 1988: 25–32.

Wardi, Anissa. "Inscriptions in the Dust: *A Gathering of Old Men* and *Beloved* as Ancestral Requiems." *African American Review* 36.1 (2002): 35–53.

Watson, Jay. "And Now What's to Do: Faulkner, Reading, and Praxis." *Faulkner Journal* 14.1 (1998): 67–74.

Weddle, David. "The Genesis of an Icon: The Creation of the Tramp" *Variety* 390.11 (2003): 4.

Weinstein, Philip. "'Make It New': Faulkner and Modernism." *A Companion to William Faulkner.* Ed. Richard C. Moreland. Malden, MA: Blackwell, 2007: 342–58.

——. "'Thinking I Was I Was Not Who Was Not Was Not Who': The Vertigo of Faulknerian Identity." *Faulkner and the Craft of Fiction.* Ed. Doreen Fowler and Ann J. Abadie. Jackson: UP of Mississippi, 1989: 172–93.

Weinstein, Sharon R. "Comedy and the Absurd in Ralph Ellison's *Invisible Man.*" *Studies in Black Literature* 3.3 (1972): 12–16.

Welty, Eudora. "Eudora Welty and Photography: An Interview." By Hunter Cole and Seetha Srinivasan. *Eudora Welty, Photographs.* Jackson: UP of Mississippi, 1989. Rpt. in *More Conversations with Eudora Welty.* Ed. Peggy Whitman Prenshaw. Jackson: UP of Mississippi, 1996: 188–213.

——. "'The Interior World': An Interview with Eudora Welty." By Charles Bunting. *Southern Review* 9 (1972): 711–35. Rpt. in *Conversations with Eudora Welty.* Ed. Peggy Whitman Prenshaw. New York: Washington Square, 1984: 40–63.

——. *Losing Battles.* New York: Vintage, 1990.

——. Preface. *One Time One Place.* Jackson: UP of Mississippi, 1996: 7–14.

Werner, Craig. "The Framing of Charles W. Chesnutt: Practical Deconstruction in the African-American Tradition." *Southern Literature and Literary Theory.* Ed. Jefferson Humphries. Athens: U of Georgia P, 1990: 339–65.

Wiggins, William H. "The Folklore Element in Ralph Ellison's *Invisible Man.*" *Afro-American Folklore: A Unique American Expereince.* Ed. George E. Carter and James R. Parker. La Crosse: U of Wisconsin-La Crosse P, 1975: 39–44.

Wilson, Charles Reagan. Introduction. *The New Regionalism.* Ed. Wilson. Jackson: UP of Mississippi, 1998: ix–xxiii.

Winther, Per. "The Ending of Ralph Ellison's *Invisible Man.*" *College Language Association Journal* 25.3 (1982): 267–87.

Wolfe, Bernard. "Uncle Remus and the Malevolent Rabbit: 'Takes a Limber-Toe Gemmun fer ter Jump Jim Crow.'" *Critical Essays on Joel Chandler Harris.* Ed. R. Bruce Bickley Jr. New York: Hall, 1981: 71–83.

Wonham, Henry B. *Mark Twain and the Tall Tale.* New York: Oxford UP, 1993.

Wright, Richard. "*Their Eyes Were Watching God.*" *Zora Neale Hurston: Critical Perspectives Past and Present.* Ed. Henry Louis Gates Jr. and K. A. Appiah. New York: Amistad, 1993: 16–17.

Yaeger, Patricia S. *Dirt and Desire: Reconstructing Southern Women's Writing, 1930–1990.* Chicago: U of Chicago P, 2000.

Yardley, Jonathan. "The Last Good One?: Eudora Welty's *Losing Battles.*" *New Republic* 162 (1970): 33–36.

Index